"A bold new book that shows how engaging with mindful awareness and compassion can allow us to step out from behind conditional and limiting self-driven narratives and into a more openhearted embrace of our lives."

—Zindel V. Segal, PhD, author of *The Mindful Way Through Depression*

"How we focus our attention can transform our lives and rewire our brains toward a healthier, more compassionate way of being. *Living with Your Heart Wide Open* is a practical, step-by-step guide that teaches us how to cultivate our awareness so that we can develop more resilient minds and enjoy lives of inner clarity and kindness. Freedom from the prison of a life on automatic pilot rests within these powerful and poetic pages."

—Daniel J. Siegel, MD, author of *Mindsight*

"*Living with Your Heart Wide Open* is both healing and awakening. By questioning and transforming the many false and negative ways we understand ourselves, we find the joy of liberation."

—Jack Kornfield, PhD, author of *The Wise Heart, A Path with Heart,* and *After the Ecstasy, the Laundry*

"The way you talk to yourself, including that murmur in the back of your head, continually shapes your outlook, your mood, and the circuits in your brain. In a warm, down-to-earth, and wonderfully useful way, *Living with Your Heart Wide Open* shows you how to change that storyline for the better for greater confidence and happiness, resilience in the face of stress, and peace of mind."

—Rick Hanson, PhD, author of *Buddha's Brain*

"A bedside book for the heart. A daily reading in healing for the part of us we have put aside for later. A letting-go of our forgetfulness of how very beautiful we essentially are. A turning toward oneself with loving-kindness."

—Stephen Levine, author of *Healing into Life and Death,*
Who Dies?, and *Meetings at the Edge*

"It has been said that the teacher who is indeed wise does not bid you to enter the house of his or her wisdom, but rather leads you to the threshold of your own. If you want to access your inner wisdom, this is a book you want by your side. If you want to live in accord with your higher power, if you want to be inspired by your experience of life, you should know that this is a book filled with reliable and authentic support."

—John Robbins, author *The Food Revolution, The New*
Good Life, and *Diet For a New America*

Living with Your Heart Wide Open

how mindfulness & compassion
can free you from unworthiness,
inadequacy & shame

Steve Flowers, MFT
Bob Stahl, PhD

New Harbinger Publications, Inc.

Publisher's Note

Distributed in Canada by Raincoast Books

Copyright © 2011 by Steve Flowers and Bob Stahl
New Harbinger Publications, Inc.
5674 Shattuck Avenue
Oakland, CA 94609
www.newharbinger.com

Cover design by Amy Shoup
Text design by Michele Waters-Kermes
Acquired by Jess O'Brien
Edited by Jasmine Star

Printed in the United States of America

Library of Congress Cataloging in Publication Data on file

Flowers, Steve.

Living with your heart wide open : how mindfulness and compassion can free you from unworthiness, loneliness, and shame / Steve Flowers and Bob Stahl ; foreword by Tara Brach.

    p. cm.

Includes bibliographical references.

ISBN 978-1-57224-935-6 (pbk.) -- ISBN 978-1-57224-936-3 (pdf e-book)

1. Attitude (Psychology) 2. Self-perception. 3. Self-confidence. I. Stahl, Bob. II. Title.

BF327.F56 2011

158.1--dc22

2011012534

14   13   12

10   9   8   7   6   5   4   3   2

To all who choose to live with their hearts wide open even as they face fear and pain.

Contents

~

Foreword

The greatest truths are too often forgotten. This book calls us back to one that is central to our happiness: If we cannot embrace our own frightened and vulnerable hearts, we cannot love our world.

Sadly, we are often at war with ourselves. More times than I can recount, people have shared with me the pain of their core beliefs. "Something is basically wrong with me," they tell me. "I don't feel worthy of love." One woman captured her pain in a way that really struck me: "I am a disgrace," she said with a mix of disgust and sorrow.

That word, "disgrace"—out of the flow of grace—speaks to the soul suffering of feeling inadequate, ashamed, or isolated. When we have turned on ourselves in harsh judgment and dislike, we lose access to our own natural intelligence, and we are cut off from our innate tenderness and openness. All that we long for—intimacy with others, peace of mind, feeling fully alive—is out of reach.

Living with Your Heart Wide Open offers a time-honored yet vibrant pathway for healing this core suffering of self-aversion. Steve Flowers and Bob Stahl are both dedicated, longtime practitioners of meditation and talented, wise mindfulness teachers. With great clarity and compassion, they introduce the principles and practices of mindfulness meditation in a way that is inviting and accessible. Their stories show us that deep emotional healing is possible, and their exercises and meditations allow us to engage directly in inner transformation. For anyone who is committed to opening beyond the trance of unworthiness, this book will be a valued friend and guide. May these teachings help you reenter the flow of grace and realize the freedom of your awakened heart.

—Tara Brach, Ph.D., author of *Radical Acceptance*

Acknowledgments

Endless acknowledgments to my kind and caring parents, Marilyn and Alvan Stahl, who have consistently embodied living to the fullest with such deep love. I want to honor my grandparents, Nettie and Ben, and Ida and Samuel, who seeded so much love into our families. Many thanks also to my brother, Barry, and sister, Kim, and their families for their loving support. Words cannot express my profound gratitude to my beloved wife, Jan, and our sons Ben and Bodhi. They keep me humble and honest, and show me the importance of family and love. Deep bows to my dharma teachers, Taungpulu Sayadaw, Hlaing Tet Sayadaw, Pakokhu Sayadaw, and Rina Sircar. I would not be on this mindful path without them.

I want to acknowledge my dear friend, beautiful wild man extraordinaire Steve Flowers, who is my coauthor in this collaboration. I am in awe of his of magnificent heart and sharp intellect.

Lastly, I want to thank all of my students, as well as my dearest dharma friends, who bring out the best in me: Mary Grace Orr, Dan Landry, Jill and Bruce Hyman, Marcy Reynolds, Jason Murphy, Skip Regan, Tom Williams, Karen Zelin, Bruce Eisendorf, Melissa Blacker, Florence Meleo-Meyer, Elisha Goldstein, Richard Shankman, Jon Kabat-Zinn, Saki Santorelli, and Vesarajja.

—Bob

This book contains the wisdom, compassion, and loving-kindness of many teachers, foremost of whom is my best friend and loving wife, Mary, whose love and generosity of spirit has transformed my life. You will find much of her wisdom and compassion in these pages. In this same spirit, I wish to acknowledge and honor my two sons, Todd and Terry, as well as my sister Kim, who have taught me the value of good faith, the power of love, and how to remain steadfast in the storms of life.

I am grateful to my clients, students, and the participants of the Mindful Living Programs retreats for the many stories of courage, redemption, and reconciliation that fill these pages. I particularly wish to extend my appreciation to Andrea Redamonte, Anne Anderson, Lorraine Van Elswyk, Rob Moore, Carrie Leontis, Kate Bartholomew, April Grossberger, and Diana Fratas for showing me how to embrace the truth of our lives and face fate with courage and self-compassion. You have taught me the power and resilience of the human spirit and how to live with an open heart no matter what life throws at you.

I extend my heartfelt gratitude to my dear friend and dharma brother Bob Stahl for his friendship and love and for so generously sharing with me his amazing gifts of wisdom and compassion. I hold dear his presence in my life. Bob has taught me what it means to be a true friend and embodies the goodness and loving-kindness that the whole world longs for.

Finally, I wish to acknowledge my dharma friends and teachers: Jon Kabat-Zinn, Saki Santorelli, Bill Knight, Nancie Brown, Gregory Kramer, Ferris Buck Urbanowski, Melissa Blacker, and Florence Meleo-Meyer, as well as my many friends and colleagues in the community of mindfulness-based stress reduction teachers. You are models for me to be all that I can be.

—Steve

We wish to offer our sincere gratitude and a deep bow to Tara Brach for her beautiful foreword, and to Rick Hanson, Jack Kornfield, Stephen Levine, John Robbins, Zindel Segal, and Dan Siegel for their thoughtful support of this book. Thank you!

—Bob and Steve

Introduction

We human beings talk to ourselves about ourselves a lot. This self-talk is rarely kind; in fact, it's often judgmental and even cruel. It's like listening to a critical sports commentator who's making a running commentary about you—your performance, your appearance, your thoughts, your life in general. It rarely shuts up, and it can make a comment about nearly everything you do or don't do. But does anybody else talk to you this way? We give this critical and prejudiced commentator a lot of credibility and listen to it intently, even though it repeats a lot of the same critical comments daily and can make us feel miserable. We allow this narrator to create and maintain our life story and define who we are. But is this self who's always being judged, or even the internal critic, really who you are? Does the commentary or even the character it describes exist anywhere other than in your head?

We call the sense of self this commentary creates the *narrative-based self*. This is not only the self that you have created and continue to maintain with your self-talk, it is most likely the self you identify with. As a result, your experience of life is based on self-references and habits of personality that are familiar to you but restrict you from discovering a deeper and more expansive experience of who you are. The narrative-based self is a mind trap. It's not who you are.

If you feel unworthy or inadequate, you are caught in this mind trap and share a misconception with a great many others who are similarly trapped in their own self-made prisons: the notion that you have a relatively fixed and stable self to begin with. But when you examine the self you've come to identify with, you'll find that it's far less substantial than you may have imagined. Who is this self? Is it your thoughts, your ideas, your beliefs? Is it your emotions, habits, behaviors, or personal history? Could it be your typical moods or personality quirks?

How about your body? Is that you? Conceptually you call it "my body," but consider it piece by piece and you'll discover that it's hard to find "you" there. Take a car for example. We might call it a Ford, but dismantle it and the Ford is nowhere to be found. Identifying with the body can create much suffering. It's subject to such vagaries of judgment. We may view it as the wrong size, shape, color, or gender. It can be too weak, too hairy, or not hairy enough. These types of judgments often originate in our culture, era, or community—but independent of these relentless judgments, we are all subject to universal conditions that nobody can escape; our bodies get hurt, get sick, grow old, and die. But look closely: Are you that finger, that hand, or that healthy head of hair? Are you the eyes that study yourself in the mirror? Who is it that is looking out from your eyes? Who listens with your ears? Who's thinking about these things?

Are you, as Descartes suggests, the one who thinks? Are you a collection of memories that thoughts maintain? Are you the story of your life? You may say, "Yes, this is who I am." Yet your thoughts and the stories they spin are also subject to change—something you'll clearly see as you develop a meditation practice. From the vantage point of mindful awareness, you recognize that the "I" character these stories create is primarily a creation of the thoughts themselves. And the self they create is actually quite malleable. It may be good or bad, depending on the mood state you happen to be in. While in one mood, you remember shining triumphs. In another mood, you'll see a long history of dismal failures. The story you identify with at any given time will offer seemingly irrefutable proof of who you are and how you are, and it can serve as a prosecutor, proving its case in front of any jury. It can prove that you are a hero or a creep, a victim or a creative genius. The more these stories are repeated, the more believable they become, and so the sense of self hardens.

Have you ever felt pretty sure that there was something wrong with you, and even if you didn't know exactly what it was, you felt fairly certain that everybody else thought so too? We've also felt this way, and it took us many years to realize that the only thing that was really wrong with us was the thought there was something wrong with us. This thought was our own self-creation. We were living in a delusion and found proof of our flawed nature in our personal histories and, seemingly, in the eyes and actions of many people we encountered. It's an idea that hasn't entirely disappeared, and either one of us can still fall under its spell in the right circumstances. We all know how easy it is to make a mistake and immediately label ourselves as terrible or stupid. Self-judgments arise so quickly and cut so deeply.

The feelings that result have many names, but all boil down to shame, self-blame, or a sense of being somehow inadequate, inferior, incomplete, insufficient, unworthy, or incompetent—as though you have a core deficit or a basic fault and something is terribly wrong with you. In this frame of mind, you may feel forsaken, left out, or rejected, or feel that you've lost your way in life.

Does this sound familiar? Do you ever notice an inner critic that hardly takes a break? Many of us are burdened with this habit of being hard on ourselves. In a mindfulness-based stress reduction class, a woman once remarked, "There's hardly been a day in my entire adult life when I haven't called myself stupid." Another person jumped in and said, "I call myself an idiot nearly every day." You might think this type of self-talk would be rare, but, sad to say, it's not. We all say these kinds of things to ourselves—a lot. If you talked to others the way you talk to yourself, you would have few friends.

This book offers a mindful path to breaking free from these habitual thought patterns. Through meditation and inquiry, you can discover where this negative self-talk comes from and why you are so judgmental toward yourself. Addressing this lack of self-compassion is essential. In a sense, our very existence is threatened by the epidemic of self-loathing. War essentially begins inside the individual, stemming from a sense of alienation and separation from the interconnectedness of life. Making peace within is one of the noblest endeavors you can pursue—for yourself, for others, and for the world.

The way to experience peace is to look into your heart, as Saint Isaac of Nineveh gently invites us to do: "Be at peace with your own soul, then heaven and earth will be at peace with you. Enter eagerly into the treasure house that is within you, [and] you will see the things that are in heaven; for there is but one single entry to them both. The ladder that leads to the Kingdom is hidden within your soul… Dive into yourself, and in your soul you will discover the stairs by which to ascend" (Oman 2000, 251).

You may have been looking for contentment in things outside of yourself. Ultimately, these can't heal the wound or fill the void. The place to look for peace is within you. In this book, we'll help you connect with your own deep inner resources for healing and self-compassion. We'll explore the causes of a sense of unworthiness and shame and guide you along a pathway to freedom. You'll learn how to use mindfulness meditation and self-inquiry to dive deeply into yourself. This is important, for this is where you'll find a ladder to ascend to wholeness and a more accepting and genuine connection with yourself, others, and the world.

Here's a preview of the terrain ahead as you embark on this important journey of healing. Throughout the book, we've interwoven key concepts from both Western and Buddhist psychology. Each offers significant benefits, and you may be surprised to discover how complementary they are. Chapters 1 and 2 provide some basic information on how a pervasive sense of unworthiness develops, primarily from the perspective of Western psychological science. Chapter 1 explores the work of self-authorship—how we construct our stories of ourselves—and how this process is influenced by early childhood development. In chapter 2, we'll look at destructive thoughts and emotions and how they manifest into a sense of self-doubt, self-blame, or inner deficiency.

Starting in chapter 3, we'll begin to bring more emphasis to Buddhist psychology and mindfulness techniques. Chapter 3 offers some basics about mindfulness, its benefits, and how to practice. Then, in chapter 4, we'll help you use mindful awareness and self-inquiry to deeply investigate the origins of painful mental and emotional habits by bringing light into the dark places of your mind and heart, including feelings of fear, self-blame, and deficiency.

In chapter 5, we'll help you cultivate self-compassion, which is key in reducing self-judgments and developing greater acceptance of yourself. Then, in chapter 6, you'll extend the healing balm of compassion and loving-kindness to yourself and outward to others and begin the important work of reconciliation, which can help you move beyond places where you've been stuck. The work you do in chapters 5 and 6 will open the door to living with your heart wide open.

In chapter 7, we'll circle back to some of the underpinnings of defining and limiting stories from a Western perspective, and also provide more mindfulness techniques for breaking free from your stories, including radical acceptance. Finally, in chapter 8, we'll take a more detailed look at some key Buddhist principles in regard to mindfulness as a way of helping you continue to develop and expand your practice once you've finished reading this book. Living with your heart wide open is a lifelong project, so we want to send you on your way with more avenues of exploration.

Every chapter will explore important facets of opening your heart to greater self-compassion and insight, and each will end with a guided meditation that you can incorporate into your daily life. All of the chapters also contain other exercises and practices, and we often encourage you to write about your experiences and insights as you engage in them. Please purchase a journal or a special notebook where you can record your thoughts and feelings throughout this journey.

We'll help you build your practice of mindfulness meditation in a stepwise fashion, starting with short, straightforward practices and building from there. At times we'll discuss the benefits of mindfulness meditation. Know that anytime you intentionally tune in to your experience in the here and now, you're practicing mindfulness meditation, so even simple practices can confer benefits. That said, the practices later in the book will provide deeper insight and more profound healing.

This book isn't meant to be read passively; it's a guidebook to an active process of learning and practice, and achieving the insight that comes from that level of engagement. Please read it slowly, taking one step at a time and savoring the journey.

For now, let's begin with a short meditation and reflection.

Mindfulness Practice: A Welcoming Meditation

Give yourself five minutes for this beginning practice. Perhaps stretch a little before you begin, then either sit or lie down. Make yourself as comfortable as possible while also remaining alert. You can close your eyes if you like, or leave them partially open if that feels more comfortable. Settle into the here and now through your breath, focusing on the sensations of breathing. The breath is an excellent vehicle for mindfulness. It's with you wherever you go, always available as a way to tune in to your experience in the moment.

Begin this meditation by taking a few moments to congratulate yourself for embarking on this journey of mindfulness and self-compassion. This is a time of new beginnings, and it's good to acknowledge this important first step on the path through and beyond feelings of unworthiness.

Next, direct your attention to how you are feeling physically, mentally, and emotionally. This may be the first time today you've slowed down to attend to yourself with attention and awareness. Feel into your body and mind and acknowledge whatever is present, whether there are feelings of tension and tightness or feelings of ease and being relaxed. Just let it all be. There may be memories of the past, plans for the future, hopes, dreams, worries, hurt feelings, joyful feelings, fears, or a myriad of other experiences.

Allow whatever is beneath the surface to rise into full awareness, and then simply acknowledge it and let it be. There's nothing you need to do, fix, analyze, or solve. Just allow yourself to be wherever you are.

As you come to an end of this meditation, congratulate yourself for taking this time to be present and directly participate in your health and well-being.

Chapter 1

~

The Fiction of Me

We do not deal much in facts when
we are contemplating ourselves.

—Mark Twain

To feel unworthy is to suffer. It feels like you're flawed and must conceal your faultiness from others or risk being shunned. But concealing, pretending, and holding yourself apart from others tends to make you feel alienated and then interpret these feelings as proof that you're flawed. This is a vicious cycle of self-doubts and self-judgments that separates you from others and prevents you from feeling whole and complete. Though you may be stuck in this self-concept, it's far more arbitrary and malleable than you may think.

Author and organizational consultant Margaret Wheatley describes this dynamic well: "We notice what we notice because of who we are. We create ourselves by what we choose to notice. Once this work of self-authorship has begun, we inhabit the world we have created. We self-seal. We don't notice anything except those things that confirm what we already think about who we already are… When we succeed in moving outside of our normal processes of self-reference and can look upon ourselves with self-awareness, then we have a chance at changing. We break the seal. We notice something new" (1999, 1). This is a power-ful insight into not only how the concept of self is perpetuated by habits of mind and perception, but also how you can free yourself and discover a much larger experience of who you are. Perhaps none of us discovers who we really are until we free ourselves from *concepts* of who we are and are not. Therefore we begin this book by exploring how the fiction of self is created and maintained.

The sense of self is formed in early childhood and gradually hardens into self-concepts and beliefs, creating a personal identity that can define and restrict you for the rest of your life. The self is conditioned primarily in early interpersonal relationships, and we then tend to see only those things that confirm who we think we are, and we screen out everything to the contrary. This is what it means to self-seal: closing off possibilities for yourself and sealing your identity, and your fate, within whatever self-construct was created when you were quite young. This self becomes a prison of beliefs that color and distort your experience of who you are.

Margaret Wheatley's quote offers insight into how we can free ourselves from this prison of funhouse mirrors with distorted reflec-tions that we mistake for reality. If you can experience yourself from the immediacy of here-and-now awareness rather than through the nar-rowed perceptions of a self created long before this moment, you can find another way of being in the world. How do you develop this here-and-now awareness? Mindfulness is the key, and as you work your way through this book, we'll offer many practices that will help you develop this perspective.

Because it's important to understand where you're starting from, in this chapter we'll explore how an identity of deficiency is constructed and persists from a Western psychological perspective as well as from the point of view of Buddhist psychology. As you learn to bring mindful awareness and inquiry into these self-limiting constructions, you're likely to discover possibilities for greater freedom and peace. It's like the Zen cartoon that shows an anguished prisoner clinging to the bars of his cell while a small door in a dark corner of his cell is clearly open. Until you let go of the bars of your prison of self and begin to explore the dark and unlit places within yourself, you can't find the door to freedom.

Self-Authorship

The stories you repeat make up your personal history and identity. They include the place and time you were born, the way it was in your family, the things that happened to you, the things you did, the things others did, your first love, and your first betrayal. It goes on and on— as long as you repeat it. When you really look at your self-stories, you may discover that they're repetitive and even arbitrary, depending on your mood. It's likely that the details don't even match up with those in the stories of your parents or closest siblings. A good question is "Who would you be without your story?" Seeing yourself without your story is an excellent way to let go of taking things personally (which can be very helpful with shame and inadequacy).

Self-authorship begins very early in life in our responses to our caregivers. If we are raised in a safe and secure environment in which we feel accepted and validated, we tend to have more self-compassion and less self-criticism (Neff and McGehee 2008). But if our caregivers are more critical or aggressive or we feel unsafe with them for any reason, we tend to become more self-critical and insecure as we grow older (Gilbert and Proctor 2006). We see ourselves in the mirrors of others' eyes and behaviors, and our stories reflect what we see there.

Who you believe you are began in your early relationships with your caregivers, and it was in these exchanges that you decided if you were worthy or unworthy, adequate or inadequate. Your story has developed within this original theme from then on. If you feel inadequate, for example, you may seek a sense of adequacy from people or things, from what you've done, or from your appearance, your talents, or your performances. This never works out. A sense of adequacy doesn't come from any of these things; it comes from who you are. This is why so many of us feel deficient and unworthy no matter what we do. We perform. We get wonderful things. We may even succeed in proving our adequacy to others, but we never quite prove it to ourselves. Shortly after every standing ovation, the sense of inadequacy returns and follows us as inexorably as a shadow.

The sense of inadequacy also follows us into our love relationships, where we tend to play out our role in some of the most dramatic ways. Surely the one who loves us will give us what we always longed for. Surely this person's love will be enough, and through it, we will finally be enough. This never quite works out either, even when our partners do their best to assure us that we're okay, or even far more than okay. In fact, the distortions of our self-authorship often manifest more dramatically in these relationships than anywhere else, due to the extraordinary perceptual distortion known as *projection*—attributing your own thoughts and judgments to others.

Projection is a kind of trance that forms the basis of all our relationships, but it's particularly prominent in our love relationships, where we may tend to project onto our partners the unpleasant thoughts and emotions we haven't yet worked through. No matter what our partners say or do, we typically believe they're expressing something else. This can drive us nuts until we start figuring out that we aren't seeing things the way they are; we're seeing things the way *we* are. But it can take a long time to gain this insight—if it ever comes at all. Most of us completely buy into the fiction of who we are, rarely noticing that we ourselves are the authors of the stories we live in.

Projection is a huge dilemma in our lives; it colors all of our relationships. It's a convoluted fiction that solidifies who we think we are and who we think everyone else is, and it drives the wedge between us ever deeper. As long as we are living within this narrative, we continue to believe we are separate and alienated from everybody else.

Why It's Never Enough

Western psychology has studied in depth how an alienated and deficient sense of self is formed in early childhood, and how failures in attachment and bonding with caregivers can create a craving for reassurance and a deep distrust of others later in life. Buddhist psychology has studied similar questions in depth, looking at how we create suffering by identifying with a fabricated self and all of its cravings, aversions, and confusion. It offers steps to help us disidentify from this separate and contracted sense of self. Both of these orientations offer understanding and tools that we can use to free ourselves from the suffering that flows from a distorted sense of self based on a faulty narrative.

When we live within unresolved childhood trauma and woundedness, it's very difficult to get glimpses of the clarity and selflessness of a here-and-now reality. We keep getting jerked back into our narrative-based self and unfinished business, no matter how desperately we'd like to leave it behind. It's like having a long bungee cord attached to your butt that won't let you move on until you've finished what you evidently need to finish. It is an enormous work for any of us to awaken from the trance we ourselves have intoned by the repetition of our stories—stories that obscure the truths and feeling we can not yet bare.

The inadequate and deficient self forged within painful interactions in early relationships will continue to plague us until we're willing to do the work of healing the child within. Mindfulness can help us open to and be near our own anguish and pain without judgment, avoidance, or pretense. But even with our growing mindfulness, this work is very difficult to do alone, particularly when working with unresolved childhood trauma. The self forged in childhood has so many defenses and self-deceptions that working alone generally isn't sufficient to access the feelings we need to feel or regulate them well enough to get free of their toxic influences. Because the sense of a deficient self is formed within interpersonal relationships, we often need to work within interpersonal relationships to understand and heal the identity we formed there. We need to cry our tears and rage our rage, and we need to find a way to reclaim all of these feelings without being overwhelmed by them. This usually involves deep personal investigation with a skilled and trusted therapist or teacher who can help us integrate and self-regulate all of the feelings we've cut ourselves off from.

We can use the wisdom and tools of Western psychology to heal the wounds of childhood and free ourselves from destructive mental and emotional patterns. And we can use the wisdom and tools of Buddhist psychology to find a larger sense of who we are that isn't driven by self-criticism and unfulfilled desire. These two orientations dovetail nicely to guide us on the path to freedom.

Many people who have practiced meditation for a long time have nonetheless done their best to avoid the difficult work of recovering and experiencing disowned feelings. It would be nice to just transcend the wounded self altogether and live in a higher state of consciousness that isn't troubled with messy things like unpleasant feelings and thoughts. But try as we might, these things keep coming up and undermining our sublime bliss. Unpleasant thoughts and feelings don't go away just because we don't like them. We have to heal the self that was created in childhood before we can enjoy the freedom of not being confined by personal narratives.

Narrative-Based Self vs. Immediacy-Based Self

Buddhist psychology asserts that we are born with a hunger for pleasure, as well as a hunger for existence and yet another hunger for nonexistence, and that these different forms of hunger are the cause of human suffering. In Western psychology, Sigmund Freud established these same human drives and acknowledged their power to cause suffering. He called the hunger for pleasure "the pleasure principle," the hunger for existence "life instinct" or "Eros," and the hunger for nonexistence "death instinct" or "Thanatos."

We don't have to look long or hard to see how these hungers create suffering in our lives. Our first experience of hunger is the hunger or will to live, which emerges immediately as a craving for physical sustenance. Immediately after birth, we cry at the top of our lungs to draw our mother's attention. We long to be reunited with her body again, and when she responds, we begin to seek for and suck from her breast. The softness of her warm skin and the nourishment of her milk are pleasurable.

We may also feel our first cravings for nonexistence very early in life. If our caregivers don't respond well to our first cravings for succor, we may eventually stop expressing this need and become withdrawn and listless. For infants, this may take the shape of failure to thrive. All of us experience this at least on occasion—times when we just want to shut down, escape, avoid, or not feel what's happening. This craving for nonexistence drives addictions of all kinds and also the urge to isolate and close ourselves off from everyone—even ourselves.

The hunger from unmet needs can form a central theme in the story you repeat to yourself, creating a narrative of a wounded self. As described above, the narrative-based self exists across time and continuously creates itself through the stories it repeats. We mistakenly believe this "self" is a somewhat permanent entity that endures through the constant changes of life. Psychologist William James characterized the narrative-based self as a construction of narratives woven together from the threads of experiences over time into a cohesive concept we reference as "me" to make sense of the "I" acting in the present moment (James 1890). The immediacy-based self, in contrast, is a creature of the here and now. It is grounded in the experience of who you are in each moment. This sense of self exists only in the present moment and therefore is ageless and timeless. It is the primary orientation from which awareness is experienced and thus is not characterized by concepts such as gender, race, religion, and personal history. As such, the immediacy-based self is not a thing but rather an active center of awareness from which you can acknowledge moment-to-moment experience. From this perspective, Descartes's famous dictum becomes "I experience what's happening, therefore I am."

Neurological research using functional magnetic resonance imaging (fMRI) has shown that these two forms of self-awareness—narrative-based self and immediacy-based self—are located in two separate areas of the brain (Farb et al. 2007). Using neuroimagery, which can detect which "self" people are operating from, this study compared novice meditators to people who had participated in an eight-week program in mindfulness meditation. When participants shifted from a narrative focus to their immediate experience, fMRIs indicated that the experienced meditators had less activity in the region associated with the narrative-based self. In other words, through the practice of mindfulness meditation we can disidentify from the self we've created with our stories and discover a new sense of self based in the present moment.

The narrative-based self lives in a continuum of past and future, and as such is the source of wanting, dissatisfaction, and judging—in short, suffering. The immediacy-based self exists only in the here and now. These two orientations in the world are fundamentally (and neurologically) different. The immediacy-based self lives with the inescapable emotional pain of being human, yet it is also present for the breeze on your face or the birdsong that you cannot feel or hear when you're preoccupied with thoughts and stories. The narrative-based self can help you avoid much of the emotional pain that's inevitable when living in the here and now, but you pay the price, as you must instead live with the suffering that self-limiting stories create.

It's important to understand the distinction between pain and suffering. Some amount of pain is inevitable in life. We'll all experience loss, setbacks, illness, and more. But suffering is different. It comprises the thoughts we heap on top of pain—thoughts that often make us feel far worse than the original pain. For example, pain is transformed into suffering when we tell ourselves things like "I'm never going to get over this. This pain is going to torture me the rest of my life."

The pathway of healing is a journey of feeling the disowned and unwanted pain that stories of unworthiness have covered and concealed. Mindfulness is a key skill for making this journey, fostering the present-moment awareness that will enable you to turn toward and be with the inevitable pain of being human. Awareness allows us to look deeply into the pain of our lives because awareness itself isn't subject to pain. It can witness pain but isn't in pain itself. It doesn't screen out feelings that seem difficult or may be unwanted; it enables you to open your heart and deeply experience what's in it.

Mindfulness and self-compassion provide a safe holding environment for your aching or raging heart—the kind of environment that a loving parent offers a child. As the restraints of your old, self-limiting stories fall away, you'll experience a measure of pain, but it's akin to the pain of childbirth, bringing a new way of being into the world. In fact, your willingness to turn toward your pain and suffering from the wide-open heart of mindfulness is a way to end suffering. In doing so, you may discover your wholeness and how to live from what is and always has been whole and complete in you, no matter what has happened in your life. This way of being is more capable of being fully present, more capable of loving and being loved. Your heart may break, but it breaks open, and this is where the light shines through.

Longing to Be Seen and Heard

When a baby is born, she cries, and something in the mother's heart immediately responds. The baby's longing to be nourished calls forth a longing in the mother to comfort and provide. The highly evolved neocortexes of both mother and baby attune and resonate together, and a built-in capacity for empathy typically guides the mother's response to her child. How the mother and other primary caregivers respond can dramatically influence the child's emotional state and later ability to emotionally self-regulate. If they don't or can't respond well to the child's emotional needs, this can contribute to feelings of unworthiness later in the child's life.

In his book *A Secure Base: Parent-Child Attachment and Healthy Human Development* (1988), psychiatrist John Bowlby discusses how central the attachment or bonding relationship between infant and caregiver is to the development of adult personality (Bowlby 1988). Bowlby believed and eventually demonstrated that the craving for attachment or emotional connectedness is an innate drive, independent of the craving for physical nourishment. He further demonstrated that how caregivers respond to the need for emotional bonding is essential to healthy social and emotional development.

Bowlby's theories correspond to parallel discoveries that had been made in the study of other primates. In a series of experiments done in the 1950s and 1960s by Harry Harlow and colleagues, infant monkeys were taken from their mothers at birth and raised with two inanimate surrogate mothers, one made of hard wire that provided the infant with a bottle of milk, and the other soft and cuddly but with no bottle. The researchers found that the infants clearly preferred to bond with the soft and cuddly "mother" even though it provided them with no food. The nourishing comfort of contact was even more important than being fed (Harlow 1959).

Bowlby and subsequent researchers in the study of attachment made similar observations about the importance of emotional nurturing and bonding in humans, and their work still provides one of the clearest explanations of how feelings of inadequacy and emptiness arise in early childhood. The research repeatedly demonstrates how important accurate empathy is for our sense of adequacy, and how we need a safe parental relationship that provides an environment where we can express our despair, anguish, and rage. If you are in some way deprived of this, your sense of self can be injured, creating what's known as a *narcissistic injury*.

The sense of self that's injured in these early relationships is the ego identity, or *conditioned self*. This is the part of your consciousness typically regarded as "me" in the narrative-based self—the very center of individuality that feels separate and distinct from everyone else. This self is the central character in the stories we tell ourselves about ourselves. For those who feel unworthy, the narcissistic injury is usually one of *deprivation*—a wound of neglect. It isn't about what happened to you; it's about what didn't happen—what you didn't receive that you needed for a safe and nurturing emotional environment. The emotional safety and accurate empathetic reflections you needed weren't there, creating a narcissistic wound from which a sense of unworthiness grows.

Paradoxically, feelings of unworthiness can also be created when a child is flooded by parental attention. This creates a type of narcissistic injury known as *engulfment*. In deprivation the child may conclude that he isn't being taken care of because there's something wrong with him. In engulfment the child may conclude that he's being taken care of so excessively because he's incapable of taking care of himself.

It may seem that this creates an impossible quandary for parents, but research shows that there is a middle way—an amount of attention that's neither too much nor too little (Winnicott 1996). The good news is, you don't have to be perfect to be an excellent parent; you only need to be good enough. In fact, good enough is perfect! This corresponds nicely with Buddhism's middle way, a concept discovered by Gautama Buddha about 2,500 years ago. There's a middle way in all things, even if we sometimes have to go to extremes to find it. As we negotiate the path to balance, it's critical that we treat ourselves with self-compassion.

Discovering a Wounded Child Within

There are many reasons why you may not have had your early interpersonal needs met, and often no one is really at fault, particularly you. Maybe you were the last of seven children and the sheer number of kids was overwhelming. Or perhaps you are a girl and your parents wanted a boy, or vice versa. You may have received that vital attention at first but for some reason it slipped away. Maybe your mom had to go back to work and no longer had enough time for you, or perhaps a baby sister or brother came along, so there wasn't as much time for you. Or maybe someone in your immediate family died or your parents got a divorce. As you can see, many of the things you might discover as you feel into your long buried feelings have nothing to do with any actual inadequacy on your part.

Oftentimes the things that lead to the development of a sense of unworthiness aren't caused by some big trauma; they're just the events of ordinary life and aren't even all that noteworthy at the time they occur. The child just feels that something isn't quite right emotionally, perhaps a vague feeling that something is absent. Trying to make sense of this feeling, the child starts trying to figure out what's wrong as soon as she can begin forming rational thoughts. But because she can't see the big picture, she's likely to mistakenly conclude that she must be lacking. This is the origin of the self-judging personal narrative. Painful questions are often too scary to verbalize: "Why don't you love me? What's wrong with me? What did I do wrong?" Yet even if unasked, these questions still beg an answer, and because nature abhors a vacuum, the child fills in the empty space with conclusions about what's wrong, often leading to the thought "There must be something wrong with me."

Though this may seem a strange conclusion, it makes sense. It's preferable to thinking that there might be something wrong with Mommy or Daddy. That thought is too terrible. Among other things it implies that the child can never get the loving attention she craves. Plus, the child can go to work on correcting herself, but there's no way to fix Mom or Dad. A great many of us arrive at feelings of unworthiness and inadequacy in exactly this way.

The motivation to do something to help or change yourself comes from a good instinct, because you really are the one most able to help yourself. But as long as you're looking for and trying to correct your deficiencies, you'll perpetuate feelings of inadequacy. In part, this is because searching for what's wrong with you is certain to yield a great many things that do indeed appear to be wrong with you, at least from the perspective of a critical mind. This approach is actually one of the well-known pitfalls of scientific investigations: The search to prove a hypothesis can bias a researcher to investigate, and sometimes recognize, only those things that support the hypothesis. The problem lies in not recognizing that our assumptions are only hypotheses, and in terms of the faulty self, we've assumed we are deficient only because we didn't get something we needed.

Longing for What We Didn't Get

As we grow into adulthood, we often end up searching for someone to give us what we didn't get as children. The absence of sufficient attention can create a gnawing hunger for outside approval. Some people become very seductive; some search for other ways to manipulate or impress. Some perform to get attention, while others become impossibly helpless. Some even try brute force and become violent in pursuit of this craving.

Though others' responses to our efforts feed our hunger, the satisfaction is only fleeting, and in the end we feel empty again. Watch a five-year-old child pursuing your attention, and you can witness the entire spectrum of human behaviors in the child's quest for satisfaction. If you look closely enough, some of these strategies may feel familiar. Even the sweetest of smiles and gestures can become a goal-oriented strategy.

What we typically don't realize as we pursue our external quest to get something we didn't get when we were little is that this convoluted effort is entirely futile. At the end of the day, no matter how well we perform or how much we get from others, it's never enough; we still end up feeling empty. The awful yet liberating truth is that the time for getting these needs met was in your childhood. You cannot get now what you didn't get then. No one else can assume the role of the loving parent you didn't have then. You may be loved and even adored in mature relationships, but that can't fill the empty space of what you didn't receive so long ago. The good news, though, is that you can learn to be with the ache in your heart with understanding and self-compassion and find peace and freedom in letting go of the desire for things to be different. Coming to terms with the way things are, with acceptance and compassion, can help you free yourself from the suffering that has imprisoned you.

Although none of us ever adequately fills the empty space in our hearts with something or someone else, the empty space itself can be something sacred in its own right. Perhaps this realization comes only after you stop thinking of the emptiness as something to be filled or hidden, and perhaps it can happen only once you come to terms with your life just as it is. It's akin to why symbols of empty space are often honored and celebrated on altars in the form of a chalice or bowl. Empty space is infinitely valuable. In the teachings of the Tao, the empty space at the center of a wheel is what makes it useful. This is also true of a vessel, a room, and even your heart and mind. Known as the sacred feminine or yin energy in Chinese philosophy, it represents the universal spirit of receptivity embodied in the accepting openness of a lake or the vibrant potentiality of a womb.

The pathway of healing involves finding ways to honor and explore the empty spaces in your heart and take ownership of the feelings you wouldn't or couldn't allow yourself to feel before. It involves feeling into the truth and contacting your hurt, for the injured place in your heart is the site where healing must occur. Rather than being something abhorrent, this wound becomes something precious to you: the heart that was once abandoned and lacking in love and compassion—from others or even yourself. You can learn how to allow disowned feelings to once again become part of you by opening to them little by little and learning to accept them with loving-kindness.

You don't have to do this alone. Often it's best to do this work in therapy or at least with the support of a trusted teacher or friend who has already traveled this difficult journey. On your own, you can begin to integrate these feelings through mindfulness meditation and self-compassion practices, yet even then it is often helpful to work through this healing process with someone else. Meditation doesn't replace therapy, but it is an invaluable adjunct to therapy. Likewise, therapy can't replace meditation, but it can support and enhance meditation practice.

When you bring compassionate awareness to the wounded heart, your narrative-based self begins to fade, and in time something new will be revealed. As you surrender into what is, you'll discover a wholeness that you couldn't know as long as you were avoiding your feelings and searching to fill the void with something from someone else.

～ Karen's Story

Karen, a wife, mother, and teacher, had all the things that are supposed to make life happy and full, but she felt as though her life was some kind of existential play. It seemed to have no meaning, no purpose, and no joy. She felt she was in a puzzle that she couldn't figure out, and finally she just quit trying. She knew she wasn't happy, but she had no idea what to do about it. Eventually, she wasn't even sure what being happy is.

She was in a decent marriage to a nice guy, but she wasn't in love with him and wasn't even sure what being in love was. She felt as though she could stay married or not, and it wouldn't make any difference to her. She didn't like her life the way it was, but didn't know if there was really anything any better. Most of the time she was so caught up in what she should do and had always done that she didn't know how she felt about anything. She was good at meeting other people's expectations, but didn't know what she wanted for herself. The last time she could remember feeling happy was when she was only about four years old.

In her meditation practice, Karen began to explore where and when she had lost her innocence and capacity for joy. She remembered living in an orphanage with many other children and being cared for by three wonderful women when she was five years old. One day a man and woman came to visit and were talking with one of Karen's "moms." She looked serious as she talked with them, and then they all stopped talking and looked at Karen. They smiled, but Karen felt weird, and when Karen's caregiver asked her to go outside and play, she knew that they were talking about her. So she didn't go outside—she stayed and listened at the door. She remembered everything as though it were yesterday. She heard her caregiver say, "She's a delightful child and we adore her—her songs, her dances, her dear laughter and sweet loving-kindness. She's an absolute jewel, but I'm afraid there are some problems with her papers."

That's when Karen lost her innocence. All of the women who cared for her in that big home were her "moms," and she loved them and loved living with them. As she listened at the door, she thought, "If they really love me, they'll keep me here." And with what she had heard, she knew she had some power to control her fate—she knew what they liked and how to please them. From then on, her smile and her songs were no longer a simple expression of joy. She learned to watch others' eyes to see if they were happy with her. She was no longer innocent; she had become purposeful. Even her laughter became another performance as she learned how to figure out what others wanted and how to give it to them. From that moment on, her life took on the purpose of keeping safe by pleasing others, and this was what governed her every choice.

Why Pleasing Others Doesn't Work in the Long Run

Pleasing others to keep ourselves safe is just one of the personality patterns created by the narrative-based or conditioned self, but it's a fairly common one. Many of us can identify with Karen. In attempting to give others what they're looking for, we start to feel like life is just a series of performances geared to fit others' expectations and make them happy. It seems like a good thing, but you can lose touch with who you are as you seek to please others. And because this kind of giving has a purpose, it creates an expectation that others will value and love you because of what you give. Unfortunately, employers, coworkers, spouses, children, other family members, and friends may consume your generosity without thinking of reciprocating, so you may end up feeling hurt, angry, and miserable—and filled with yet more self-loathing—as you experience failure and disappointment again and again.

If you can follow the thread of your own process of self-authorship, you may find in yourself a very young child still living out self-protection strategies that arose long ago. You are holding one end of this thread right now. It's the way you are—the way you do things. It's your personality and it's got a particular style intended to get something from or get away from significant others in your life. Follow the thread and you will discover how you've created the sense of self that you are living in today. Yet this thread is something spun by your internal narrative, and remaining attached to it is neither inevitable nor inescapable.

As you follow this thread to see how your narrative developed, you may become angry. You may feel like blaming those who were supposed to take better care of you. That's okay. These moments of anger and hurt may help you reclaim feelings that you've lost touch with. That said, it's important to acknowledge at the beginning of this inner exploration that the goal is not to find fault or place blame, but only to better understand how you came to feel deficient and unworthy.

Of course, there are horrible parenting failures that deeply injure children, and these kinds of traumatic injuries are often passed down from generation to generation until someone in the succession of wounded innocents breaks the chain and travels the path to healing. But often even parents who mean to do the best by their children find it very difficult to discern the middle way, of neither too much nor too little attention. Parents can fail even when trying to do the right thing. For those who were neglected in childhood, it can be all too easy to engulf their children with too much love, and for those who were engulfed in childhood, it's all too easy to be too withholding.

Buddhist Perspectives on the Self

Having looked at how a sense of inadequacy arises due to influences on childhood development, let's now explore this feeling from the perspective of Buddhist psychology. When the Dalai Lama first heard that Westerners often feel a tremendous lack of self-worth or self-esteem, he was surprised and puzzled. It took a great deal of explanation for him to understand this nemesis of Western civilization. It was hard for him to conceive that we could feel so deficient (Goleman 2003).

In *Buddha's Brain*, Rick Hanson and Richard Mendius say that "from a neurological standpoint, the everyday feeling of being a unified self is an utter illusion: the apparently coherent and solid 'I' is actually built from many subsystems and sub-subsystems over the course of development, with no fixed center, and the fundamental sense that there is a subject of experience is fabricated from myriad, disparate moments of subjectivity" (2009, 211). It may be tempting to think that the self must be your thoughts, but these too are always changing and rather arbitrary. Interestingly, in Buddhist psychology the mind is considered to be one of the sense organs. Just as the nose smells, the eyes see, the tongue tastes, the ears hear, and the body feels, the mind thinks. This is just what it does—it's a mental processing plant, but it's not you.

Perhaps it's akin to hardware and software. Being a human being means you have hardware that's equipped with the apparatus of a mind, body, and senses, but the lens through which you see yourself and the world is software that's been programmed with self-definitions of who you think you are and further reinforced by those close to you. This essentially arbitrary self-definition is dependent on your early childhood experiences and perpetuated by your self-story and the expectations of others.

Buddhist psychology speaks of this confusion around self as similar to watching a movie and getting caught up in the drama. Yet when broken down, the reality is one single frame at a time. Because the mind likes continuity, it uses a self-story to link multiple but separate experiences of self into a cohesive story. But a fixed and stable self is an illusion. In this way, imposing a story about your deficiency on your life takes a subjective experience from the past and projects it out into the future.

But what if that's the way it is?

23

From the point of view of Buddhist psychology, you can free yourself from suffering and the limitations of the narrative-based self only when you awaken from the illusions this self creates. In the words of Margaret Wheatley, quoted at the beginning of this chapter, this awakening allows you to "break the seal [and] notice something new" (1999, 1). It frees you from the story that keeps you trapped in a constricted sense of self, and only then can you outgrow the self you have created. As you build your mindfulness meditation practice, you'll develop the deep insight into the workings of your mind that will allow you to deconstruct your conditioned self. The hurt, anger, or unworthiness you feel, and even the personality that pursues satisfaction of its cravings, is only the result of your early programming. They are not you. Your wholeness and deep connection to every other living being has always been present; it's just that you've been caught up in other things and couldn't see it.

Buddhist psychology regards ignorance as the source of all suffering. And of all forms of ignorance, it considers thinking that you're a separate self to be the first and worst kind. This is the ultimate source of all the mind traps of hunger and fear. The antidote is mindfulness practice, which allows you to witness the coming and going of thoughts and emotions and to recognize how you create a deficient sense of self through a personal narrative of thoughts and emotions focused on "I," "me," or "mine." You'll come to see how you create a sense of being faulty through thoughts like "I wish I were a better person," "I just don't belong anywhere," or "What's wrong with me?"

Buying into the fiction of a stable and unchanging self is the greatest trap for subjecting yourself to destructive emotions, and often the most difficult to extricate yourself from. At first the realization that the self in your story is no more than a fabrication of your own mind may be more than a little disorienting, not to mention distressing. But if you can stay with this and continue to investigate it, you'll find that this insight is extremely liberating and can completely change your orientation and way of being in the world. When you let go of your attachment to a fixed and separate self, you'll get your first taste of true freedom. To get you started on your healing journey, we'll close this chapter with a meditation that can help you learn to live in the present moment.

Mindfulness Practice: Meditation on the Breath

If you're new to meditation, we'd like to offer you a few general pointers on body position and other physical aspects of practice. Sitting is generally preferable, but you can also lie down if you're able to remain alert, and you can even stand if you like. In any position, keep your head, neck, and body somewhat aligned. If you sit, aim for a posture that's self-supporting, rather than leaning back against a chair, and make sure your legs can rest comfortably, without requiring muscle tension to hold them in place. Find a place where you can rest your hands. Look for your middle way—not too tight and not too loose, a position where you can be comfortable and alert for the entire practice. Feel free to have your eyes closed or partially open—whichever you feel most at ease with. If you keep your eyes partially open, your gaze should be more inward, on whatever you're focusing on, rather than outward, where you may get lost in what you're seeing. If you find yourself getting sleepy, you might want to open your eyes or stand up.

The breath is an excellent focus for mindfulness practice. Your breath is always there, always coming and going. It's also something that's available to you anytime, anywhere.

Give yourself ten to fifteen minutes for this practice.

Begin by bringing your attention to the breath in either your nostrils or your belly—wherever you feel it most distinctly. As you breathe in, be aware of breathing in, and as you breathe out, be aware of breathing out. Let the breath come and go as it will, normally and naturally. Let the felt sense of the breath coming and going be your way to be present for the full duration of the in breath and the full duration of the out breath. Letting yourself be...

There's no need to visualize anything or regulate the breath in any way. There's no need to engage thoughts or words or phrases of any kind. Just be mindful of breathing in and breathing out, without judgment, without striving. Just watch the breath ebbing and flowing like waves in the sea.

Notice the inevitable moments when your attention wanders from the breath. When this happens, don't criticize or berate yourself. Simply acknowledge where you went, perhaps into the future or the past, or engaging in some kind of judging. Just return to the breath, again and again, every time you leave it.

There's nothing to accomplish, nothing to pursue, nothing to do but simply sit and be where you are, noticing your breathing. Living your life one inhalation and one exhalation at a time…

As you come to an end of this meditation, please extend some appreciation and congratulations to yourself for giving yourself this gift of mindfulness.

Savoring This Journey

In this chapter you learned a foundational mindfulness practice: meditating on the breath. This is a powerful way to ground yourself in the present moment. Remember, your breath is always there—always available as a way to bring yourself back into the here and now. We highly recommend practicing mindful breathing daily, and making this a lifelong practice. Try doing a few minutes of mindful breathing before you even get out of bed in the morning, as a way to set the tone for your day, and to establish an intention to live more mindfully. Focusing on the breath can also bring you a measure of calm in difficult times. Anytime you feel yourself becoming stressed, upset, or beset by difficult thoughts or emotions, pause for a few mindful breaths. This will create a little space and may allow you to choose a different way of responding to the situation.

Chapter 2

~

Choosing How You Look at Things

If you are distressed by anything external, the pain is not due to the thing itself but to your estimate of it; and this you have the power to revoke at any moment.

—Marcus Aurelius

When Christine's husband left her for a younger woman, her self-concept plummeted. As she stood in front of the mirror, she thought she looked fat and ugly. She hated her face, her hair, and everything about the way she looked. She felt like she was back in eighth grade again, when she was short, wore thick glasses, had braces on her teeth, and was deathly afraid of every boy in school. "It's no wonder he chose her," she cried. "I'm disgusting and boring." She shamed herself for months.

Then she learned that her husband had slept with many other women while he was married to her, and that he was already cheating on his new girlfriend too. It dawned on her that his infidelity had nothing to do with her; it was about him, about a compulsive sexual addiction he'd been hiding for years. It was still devastating to suffer the loss of her marriage, but she realized that all of the punishing judgments and self-blame she'd heaped on herself were entirely unwarranted and only added to her suffering. As she laid down her burden of shame, she was surprised to find that she actually pitied her husband for losing her—a far cry from self-pity and blaming herself for losing him. Her marriage was lost, but she'd reclaimed herself, and her path of healing had begun.

Thoughts and emotions are the primary building blocks of the story of deficiency you identify with. After a thought about yourself becomes embedded in your mind, you filter your perceptions through the magical lens of interpretation, ensuring that you see only what you already believe about who you are. It doesn't have to be even remotely true; you just have to believe it. As a result, a thought like "I'm deficient and unworthy of love" may become the primary assumption around which you construct your world.

Thoughts and emotions are deeply entangled. Sometimes thoughts spur emotions, and sometimes emotions spur thoughts. Judgmental thoughts can create guilty feelings. Guilty feelings can lead to self-blaming thoughts. It doesn't matter which precedes or follows the other; in the end some combination of thoughts and feelings provides the building materials for constructing your sense of self. You fabricate your life, your world, your heaven or hell with these fleeting, amorphous things called thoughts and feelings, but what are they, really? They have no inherent truth or substance, yet you use them to create all that you deem good or bad, right or wrong, worthy or unworthy. You can't hold them in your hand, though your hand may sweat because of them. They have no weight, but they can become so heavy that they crush you into immobility. In this chapter we'll examine the role of thoughts and emotions in creating a conditioned self that holds itself separate from everyone else.

Thoughts That Construct the Deficient Sense of Self

Thoughts are mental symbols of the world in and around us. They're useful for representing the world, but they can create enormous suffering when we assume that they're accurate. They aren't. Like Christine, we all have the capacity to make ourselves absolutely miserable with thoughts that have nothing to do with reality. It may seem strange, but ascribing inaccurate judgments and interpretations (which are just thoughts) to our experience is a frequent and universal human pastime.

Reality Is Relative

We usually don't see that which is before us; we see our interpretations of what is before us. These interpretations transform our perceptions to fit our beliefs and expectations. In essence, we see the world as we think it is. In this way, a beautiful woman who is filled with negative self-judgments can look in the mirror and see someone hideous looking back at her. What color are the lenses you're looking through? Whatever it may be, your whole world will become that color.

Mindfulness can help you investigate how you look at things, and particularly how you look at yourself. When you witness your habitual ways of thinking about yourself, you'll get some clues about how your thoughts are shaping your self-concept. You'll discover that certain story lines predominate in your personal narrative of you. Be especially alert to phrases that begin with "I always" or "I never." These usually indicate that you've just reinforced an important element of your self-story.

Mindful awareness will help you take this entire process off of automatic pilot and investigate how you think, and therefore how you perceive. In time, you'll come to see that your thoughts don't necessarily represent reality but may actually be constructing it. As it turns out, reality is relative. The world and everything in it, including your sense of self, transforms in relation to how you look at it.

Certain thoughts lead to predictable emotions; it's a process that's familiar to all of us. If a thought of loving-kindness is present, happiness occurs. If a self-blaming thought is present, guilt occurs. Thoughts are the central building blocks of many mental afflictions, including a pervasive sense of worthlessness, and it's important to recognize the patterns of thought that create suffering in our lives. The key is to find a perspective from which you can make thoughts themselves an object of awareness and take them off of automatic pilot. Once you are no longer kneeling at the altar of thought, these arbitrary and capricious representations of reality can no longer rule your life. They'll lose their power to sweep you into misery.

The modern psychologies of the West have developed interventions to repair problems with the self, using techniques such as investigating how we think and learning skills to change dysfunctional thinking. Buddhist psychology also acknowledges that thoughts create suffering, but rather than working to change thoughts, this approach considers the act of witnessing thoughts without getting caught up in them to be an effective way to dispel their power. The part of you that witnesses thoughts is separate and distinct from self-limiting interpretations, and therefore isn't defined by them. This is one of the most valuable gifts of mindful awareness. The following exercise will help you develop the ability to witness and acknowledge your thoughts without regarding them as true or accurate reflections of reality.

Exercise: Investigating Thoughts and Letting Them Be

By now it should be clear: You don't have to fall for all of your interpretations hook, line, and sinker. You don't have to believe all of your thoughts. The next time you find yourself feeling inadequate or unworthy, take a few mindful breaths and then use the following technique to take a closer look at a thought that's feeding these feelings.

> Consider whether this thought is true or even pertinent, and notice how believing this thought makes you feel emotionally.
> Notice how believing this thought makes you feel physically. For about five minutes, stay with your physical sensations as best you can. Every time your mind returns to the thought,

or related thoughts, redirect it back to sensations, even unpleasant sensations. Center your awareness in your body and simply let the thoughts be.

Staying grounded in your body and the sensations of the here and now, consciously turn toward the thought. Ask yourself, "How would I feel if I simply let this thought be whenever it arises? How would I feel if I let this thought come and go without getting involved in it?"

Ask yourself, "What within me is asking for acceptance and compassion?" Spend as long as you like with this question.

Take a little time to write in your journal about what you discover with this practice, exploring how you feel when you witness yourself with kindness rather than criticism.

This technique is a simple yet powerful way to work with thoughts and can tease out the distorted interpretations you use to create your sense of self. Making thoughts themselves the object of awareness can undermine the power of self-blaming and self-shaming thoughts. You can also use this technique with other types of thoughts. As you practice it, you may be surprised to discover how many things you think you know that you don't really know for certain.

Judging

Of all the wondrous array of thoughts that are possible, negative judgments about ourselves and others are one of the mind's favorites. It's as if the human brain has a hyperactive gland that secretes judgments, just like the adrenal gland secretes adrenaline. Negative and reactive judgments can arise instantaneously and in regard to almost anything. Sometimes they focus almost exclusively on you, and sometimes almost exclusively on others.

Exercise: Investigating Judgments

If you allow critical judgments to remain unexamined, they can come to occupy many of your thoughts and emotions, and even your dreams. But if you examine them, you'll find repetitive themes that are connected to earlier life events and discover that even your judgments regarding others are often rooted in self-judgment or events that happened earlier in your life—sometimes when you were very young. It's a good practice to question all of your judgments, and this exercise will help you do exactly that. Give yourself about thirty minutes for this exercise.

Spend at least five minutes practicing mindful breathing.

Next, see if you can remember a strong judgment you've had about yourself or someone else in the last few days.

As you feel into the judgment, notice if there's a physical component—something you feel in your body. Spend at least five minutes investigating the way your body feels as you reflect on this judgment.

What thoughts accompany the judgment? Was there anything automatic in the way this judgment came up? For example, was the judgment a reaction to something or someone? Spend at least five minutes investigating the thoughts that arise in relation to this judgment.

What are the emotions that accompany the judgment? For example, some judgments may call forth anger, whereas others evoke shame and yet others evoke compassion. Spend at least five minutes investigating the emotions that arise in relation to this judgment.

Notice that the part of you that is investigating this judgment is not itself judging anything; it's simply observing bodily sensations, thoughts, and emotions with dispassionate curiosity.

Now consider whether this kind of judgment has come up before. Does it come up often? If so, do you have any sense of why you have this strong and automatic reaction? Does it isolate you from others or make you feel more connected? Can you sense where it comes from? Please spend at least five minutes reflecting on the historical associations related to this judgment.

Take a little time to write in your journal about what came up for you as you investigated your judgments. What sorts of physical sensations and emotions were associated with different judgments? Did you discover any associations between judgments and earlier life events?

You can also investigate judgments in the moment. Try this exercise the next time you find you're having a strong critical reaction toward someone. See if you can notice what happens in your body, how your body feels. Then imagine that you're leaning toward the other person with your index finger pointing at the person and a tense, mean look on your face (sometimes you might even actually catch yourself in this posture). Notice that when you point at others, you have three other fingers pointed back at yourself. Follow them back to yourself and investigate how this judgment toward someone else has something to do with you. Many judgmental thoughts about others have their origins in painful events earlier in life. These kinds of judgments call for deep personal inquiry.

∼ Mike's Story

For most of his life Mike felt a strong aversion to anger and was judgmental of people who were angry, especially when their anger was filling up his environment. This was a problem in his marriage, because his wife had reclaimed the power and sovereignty she had lost in childhood through her anger. For her, anger was a good thing, but for Mike her anger was a bad thing—and one of the few things that provoked his own anger in their relationship.

One evening he was once again growing angry at her for being angry and decided to take a shower instead of giving voice to the critical and angry thoughts he was thinking. Feeling the warm water on his body brought him away from his critical mental dialogue and back to his here-and-now self and his own feelings. He decided to investigate his reactive anger more deeply, and as the feelings underneath his anger began to emerge, he began to feel really scared and sad. Feeling into that fear, it exploded into terror and helplessness and he collapsed on the shower floor, overcome with a sense of horror he hadn't felt since he was ten years old. A doorway into his heart had opened, and feelings he had been repressing for years by avoiding anger came pouring though him as his heart tore open even more.

He remembered being in another shower as a boy and hearing his parents, beyond the door, screaming and breaking things—something they did a lot, with terrible cruelty and violence, and he felt helpless and vulnerable. It had been decades since he had felt these things, and he began to sob.

He always tried to make his parents stop, but his little voice was drowned out by their roaring profanity. They never stopped, and in their rage they hurt one another and Mike deeply. He cried in the shower as this old terror erupted from his core, and then he realized that this was where his reactive judgments about anger were oozing from. His heart filled with compassion and love for the boy who was hurt in those battles, and from that place he sought out his wife to let her know what he had learned. He made a commitment to keep this insight in front of him, and to learn to honor her anger. They cried together.

Defusing Judgments

Judgments are like bombs that can be triggered by life events. Imagine that you're in the grocery store and see a mother angrily slap her daughter's leg, and the child looks humiliated when she sees you watching. Or imagine that someone cuts in front of you near an intersection, so that you get stuck at the stoplight while he drives on. Picture a scenario in which your spouse criticizes your house cleaning. These types of events can trigger strong judgments and anger.

Negative judgments can explode in our minds at any moment and overwhelm us with immediate and emotionally overwhelming condemnations of others or ourselves. The body contracts, blood pressure rises, and the breath moves up into the chest and becomes shallow and rapid. The fight-or-flight response has been triggered, and an urge to say or do something floods you. In these moments, regrettable words can leap out of your mouth and injure others, and even yourself. Many of us have extremely short fuses when similar triggering events occur again and again, and our reactions can be like bombs that go off almost instantaneously.

The bombs with the shortest fuses are often found in our relationships with other people. Politicians and strangers in traffic are a common source of small, frequent reactions that come and go like firecrackers. But our love relationships can set off huge explosive reactions that can create enormous suffering for years. Careless words can cut deeply and leave scars that never go away. Because love relationships are so intimate, they have the capacity to call forth emotional reactions that are tied to earlier traumatic interpersonal events. This is one reason why these relationships are so rife with projections. Projections are ego defense mechanisms that operate mostly unconsciously and impose on current relationships the emotional injuries from earlier close relationships, such as with your mother, your father, or your first love. Although we're usually unaware of our projections, we can learn a great deal about them if we're willing to investigate our reactive judgments with an intention to defuse them.

Exercise: Defusing Judgments

This practice will help you strengthen your ability to defuse judgments by bringing awareness and compassion to aversive feelings. An inextricable part of developing this skill is to deliberately make contact with difficult feelings. However, if at any point this mindful exploration becomes too disturbing, return to feeling your breath in your belly. This is a home base you can return to throughout the exercise until you feel grounded, and then you can be with the difficult feeling once again and try to stay with it. Also, please note that defusing a judgment doesn't mean getting rid of it; it means neutralizing it or removing its sting.

Sit comfortably and begin by bringing your full attention to the breath coming and going in your belly. If you like, place your hand on your belly and feel it rising with the in breath and falling with the out breath. Stay with this practice as long as you like before proceeding.

Recall the judgment you explored in the previous exercise, or any other judgment that you'd like to explore and defuse. First note who or what you were judging. Notice the reactive thoughts and emotions connected to the judgment, including any stories, beliefs, or memories that emerge. What are you judging about this event and the people involved in it? Be open to and welcome the emotions that arise in this exploration, and respond to these feelings with kindness and self-compassion. Note that these feelings and memories are connected to the judgment yet separate from it.

Feel the bodily sensations connected to the memories and emotions that came up as you considered your judgment, and move back and forth between these sensations and the thoughts and emotions a few times. Notice the difference between the mental formations (thoughts, emotions, memories) and the sensory formations (experiences of sight, sound, touch, smell, and taste). In this way, you can use the body to anchor in the here and now and defuse difficult thoughts and emotions, removing some of their charge.

Next, shift away from this focus on the judgment and the mental and physical phenomena associated with it and take a few minutes to reflect on the part of you that just explored these mental, emotional, and physical states—a part of your consciousness you can think of as the observing or witnessing awareness. Notice that the part of you that is aware of judging is curious but not itself judgmental. Awareness can notice the judging and the mental and physical phenomena associated with it without getting caught up in them. As you reflect on this awareness, notice if your heart softens in any way and you feel a little less critical.

From this perspective you can extend love and compassion to yourself for whatever comes up for you in this mindful reflection. You may also extend compassion and loving-kindness to whomever you may have been judging. What are the words and gestures you would like to offer to yourself for any pain or unhappiness that came up? What would you say to someone you love who was feeling this way?

Notice what happens in your body and mind as you offer these expressions of compassion and loving-kindness. Pay attention to what comes up for you physically, mentally, and emotionally, and look for connections between mental events and their emotional or physical counterparts. For example, self-compassion may create a feeling of release in the chest, or self-forgiveness may allow the belly to soften.

Return to conscious breathing, bringing your full attention to the breath coming and going in your belly for a few moments before concluding this exercise.

Take some time to write in your journal about the thoughts and feelings you experienced in this exercise. Write about your reflections on the questions above as specifically as possible. Bring particular attention to reactive judgments and any historical associations they may have in your life, as well as any sensations associated with the judgments you worked with. What words of self-compassion and loving-kindness came up for you in this exercise? How did the sensations associated with judgments change when you offered yourself words of loving-kindness and compassion?

Wisdom grows from the "one step removed" kind of awareness cultivated by this practice. Indeed, simply naming a thing ("judgment") is a powerful first step toward defusing it. Sometimes our thoughts and feelings create reactive judgments simply because we refuse to acknowledge or feel them.

Ruminating

Sometimes it isn't thoughts that create so much trouble; it's thinking itself. And even then, it isn't that thinking about something that upsets you is a bad thing in its own right; it's just that sometimes once the mind gets going, it's hard to stop. This type of repetitive thinking, or rumination, is a common problem. Most of us have experienced it when trying to get to sleep on the eve of a big event. It can become a defining and central characteristic for those with a sense of inadequacy, as well as in mental disorders such as anxiety, depression, and obsessive-compulsive disorder. When cows ruminate, they regurgitate the grass they ate earlier and chew it again, which, we are told by farmer friends, smells terrible. This may sound disgusting, but it's actually a lot like what we do when we ruminate (maybe explaining why ruminating is sometimes called "stinking thinking"). But not only does our rumination fail to nourish us, we also have the added problem of rehashing what has already happened again and again, and may even ruminate on what didn't happen or what may or may not happen. Rumination can create enormous suffering.

Learning to be aware of thoughts rather than mindlessly being seduced into believing you *are* your thoughts is one way out of rumination. Take a moment to quietly observe your mind's working, and simply say to yourself, "Oh, that's a thought, and that's another thought, and that's another thought." Then take it a step further and ask yourself, "Who is witnessing these thoughts? Who is watching them come and go?" These simple approaches are the foundation of mindfulness practices that can greatly enhance your ability to attend to what you're thinking without identifying with the thoughts, the self that thoughts create, or even the act of thinking itself. They will help you refine the awareness that witnesses thoughts but isn't defined by them. Thoughts happen. With mindful awareness, you can let them happen and not get too entangled with them.

Emotions That Construct the Identity of Deficiency

All human beings have emotions, and none of those emotions is beneficial or destructive in its own right. But as with thoughts, we can create a great deal of suffering depending on how we respond to our emotions. The Gnostic Gospel of Thomas quotes Jesus as saying, "If you bring forth what is within you, what you bring forth will save you. If you do not bring forth what is within you, what you do not bring forth will destroy you" (45:29-33). This is certainly true of emotions, which can become destructive when we repress them. Yet those same emotions can become a source of healing when we feel into them and bring them forth, even when they're unpleasant. We must find a way to feel our anger, fear, shame, and all of the other feelings that are difficult for us. This calls for one of the central attitudes of mindfulness: being present with and acknowledging even those feelings (and thoughts) we don't like or don't want. This doesn't mean passively submitting to difficult emotions and allowing them to pummel us, or others. It means being with these feelings with the patience, compassion, and acceptance fostered by mindfulness meditation.

In early childhood, we learned which feelings others preferred us to feel and express and which they discouraged. If your parents couldn't tolerate your anger, you probably learned to block it and stuff it. If they couldn't acknowledge your fear, your pain, or even your excitement, you might have avoided or closed off these emotions too. Sometimes simply naming a difficult emotion defuses it and helps us deal with it more constructively. Try it and see. When an emotion arises, say to yourself, "It's just fear [sadness, anger, grief, shame, guilt, loneliness, confusion, rage, hostility, or whatever]. It's just an unpleasant emotion." Remind yourself that these emotions are universal—felt in all cultures throughout history, and by even the youngest babies.

As with thoughts, with emotions the key is to feel and acknowledge them without pushing them away, identifying with them, or letting them carry you away. Mindfulness meditation is immensely helpful here. It can help you see the habitual ways in which you try to avoid a variety of things, including painful emotions. It also helps you develop the capacity to welcome and allow the emotions you've tried to avoid. This is important, as emotions play a huge role in how we feel about ourselves and connect with one another, and can also trump thoughts entirely in the thought/emotion equation of unworthiness.

With mindfulness and self-compassion, you can learn to let emotions come and go, simply acknowledging them as pleasant, unpleasant, or neutral. Even if you don't like them or don't want them, you must find some way to feel them and let them be. If stuffed and denied for long enough, they can become all-consuming and create a great deal of suffering in your life. As with thoughts, mindfulness will help you see them as just emotions, a part of your consciousness but not all of your consciousness. It's important to learn how to regulate difficult emotions, but you can do that only by turning toward them and staying with them long enough to know them deeply. In time, difficult emotions become just anger, just fear, or just shame, rather than a story line that defines who you are. When you allow them and let them be, emotions come and go. In later chapters, we'll offer many skills and approaches to help you to understand, integrate, and regulate difficult emotions.

Part of understanding emotions is looking at where they come from. They may be triggered by thoughts or perceptions, but sometimes they don't seem to have a clear or obvious cause. Another part of understanding emotions is attending to how they affect you. Some emotions seem to linger in the mind or body for many years; examples would be fear of a parent or resentment of a spouse or partner who betrayed you.

Exercise: Experiencing Emotions in the Body

If you attend closely to your emotional states, you'll find that they often trigger sensations in your body. Some of these are universal. For example, anger energizes our hands and arms to prepare us to fight, and fear sends blood into our legs to prepare us for flight (Dalai Lama and Ekman 2008). Some physical responses are more idiosyncratic, like blushing when embarrassed or ashamed, or getting sweaty hands or cold feet when frightened. One of the hallmarks of emotions is their physiological signatures, which can inform others about how we're feeling. This allows us to build connections with one another (or not), on the basis of the emotions we read in others' faces and feel in their presence.

> Sit comfortably and begin by bringing your full attention to the breath in your belly, allowing the breath to come and go normally and naturally. Stay present with your breath until you feel fully grounded in the here and now.
>
> Expand your attention to feel the body as a whole, from the top of your head to the tip of your toes. Staying in touch with your body, recall one of the less difficult emotions from the exercise on defusing judgments, earlier in this chapter, along with the stories and beliefs associated with that emotion. Notice what happens in the body as you feel this emotion. Simply sit with this sensation as best you can, with curiosity and compassion. Spend at least five minutes in this investigation.
>
> Let these reflections go, and return to awareness of the breath in your belly, being present and letting yourself be. From this place, extend appreciation to yourself for engaging in this mindful exploration. Also extend self-compassion for whatever difficult thoughts and feelings emerged, placing your hand on any parts of the body that resonated with the emotion and holding yourself with loving-kindness.

Take some time to write in your journal about what you experienced in this exercise. What physical sensations were associated with the emotion you explored? How did the emotion and related sensations change as you extended compassion to yourself?

You can work with all difficult and unpleasant emotions in this way, whenever they come up for you. The discoveries you make can help you respond rather than react the next time you find yourself in the grip of strong emotions.

Sensing Your Emotions

Many people find that focusing on the physical sensations connected to difficult emotions helps them defuse these emotions and gradually integrate them. However, it's important to note that integrating and regulating difficult emotions can be a very challenging and long-term process that requires much patience and self-compassion. Give yourself a lot of time and space for this work.

Also be aware that emotions can impel you into actions that are conditioned and automatic, and these automatic reactions are often the greatest cause of suffering in your life and the lives of those around you. Adding to the problem, emotions typically fly up before you can even notice that they're coming. Usually you'll notice an emotion only after you're in it. Furthermore, once you're in the grip of an emotion, it's likely that you'll notice only things that support that emotion and screen out those that don't.

This is why it's so helpful to explore how you experience emotions in your body, as in the preceding exercise. Sensations that are connected to emotions can become a signal that you're in the grip of an emotion before you automatically react to it, so that you can bring attention and intention to responding to the emotional signal more deliberately. If you know that tightness in your jaw is a sign that you may be angry, this can help you pause and reflect before acting. You may not be able to intervene before you become emotional, but with mindfulness and self-compassion you can learn to respond to emotions skillfully, rather than reacting automatically.

An oft-repeated quote succinctly describes this dynamic: "Between stimulus and response, there is a space. In that space lies our freedom and our power to choose our response" (Pattakos 2008, viii). Mindfulness is the space between the stimulus and the response that allows you to make more conscious and deliberate choices when you're emotional.

Moods

Intense emotions that are triggered again and again, either by a repeated event or by ruminating on an event, can become embedded as a mood, which can be considered an enduring emotional state. Sometimes moods last just a few hours, but other times we may get stuck in moods for days or longer, and some people may be more prone to this. If you entertain a mood long enough, it can color your life with such deep hues that it washes out any new information that's contrary to what you expect. For example, newlyweds in a giddy mood can virtually float through delays and other vagaries of travel that would normally drive them nuts with exasperation.

One of the ways that emotions and moods differ is that you can usually figure out what triggered an emotion, but you may not be able to figure out what created a mood. After all, not all newlyweds find themselves in a giddy mood—some are surprised to discover themselves anxious and pensive and may not understand why they feel this way. This is because moods restrict our access to past knowledge, so we have difficulty taking in new information that doesn't reinforce and validate what we're feeling. For example, a new bride who's in a pensive mood may look at the things her husband is taking delight in and wonder what's so delightful.

If you live in a mood long enough, it can crystallize into a story line or character trait you identify with and then believe, such as "I'm an unhappy and unpopular person, and no one takes much interest in me." This may just be a story about yourself that you believe even though it has nothing to do with who you really are. For example, one of Winnie-the-Pooh's most loveable and famous friends, Eeyore the donkey, is stuck in a dismal and gloomy mood that has become his attitude toward life. He entirely believes the story line that nobody cares about him, even though everyone around him loves him.

Emotional Set Points

The Dalai Lama has said that happiness isn't a fixed characteristic, but rather is something that can be enhanced through mental training (Dalai Lama and Cutler 1998). This assertion, which comes from his own deep commitment to the practice of meditation and compassion, has been passed down through the ages in the teachings of Buddhism and is also supported by contemporary neuroscience. We all have *emotional set points*. These are sort of like thermostat settings for our emotions. They influence when an individual will typically be overcome by an emotion such as anger or happiness, how extreme the emotional reaction will be, and how long it will last.

Although these set points have been considered to be relatively stable throughout a person's lifetime, Richard Davidson, one of the foremost neuroscientists studying emotions, has found that meditation practice can induce long-lasting and beneficial changes in the brain, including altering emotional set points (Davidson 2009). In fact, these set points can be changed for the better with mindfulness and compassion practices in as little as eight weeks. In other words, your brain's set point for happiness (or any other emotion) is up to you. Likewise, a study currently being conducted by researchers at Harvard is documenting significant positive correlations between feelings of happiness and living in the here and now. The more the study subjects are focused on the present moment, the happier they feel, and the more their minds wander, the more unhappy they feel (Killingsworth and Gilbert 2010). Isn't it wonderful that modern science is validating what the ancient psychology of Buddhism has encouraged for some 2,500 years?

Self-Fulfilling Prophesy

Once you've formed a limited and limiting sense of self from powerful emotions like shame, you'll seek ways to recreate these emotions to maintain that identity. This is called emotional scripting by researcher Paul Ekman (Dalai Lama and Ekman 2008), and it explains how the profound emotional experiences of childhood can become like the script of a play that you repeatedly impose on your life experiences. Take Mike's story; he imposed his emotional script of terror and helplessness onto his love relationships from high school on, a script that called forth feelings of being inadequate, helpless, and unsafe. So all these years later, whenever his wife becomes angry he has the same awful feelings that his parents' behavior evoked and reacts as though she is dangerous and will hurt him.

Another term for this is *self-fulfilling prophecy*. Whatever you call it, it's one of the ways we create and recreate the stories we live in. We can do this with any of our emotions and moods. For example, you might conclude that you're inherently unlovable and therefore decide to not risk exposing your supposedly deficient and empty character to others for fear of their rejection. Instead, you give them an improved but false version of yourself. However, this kind of hiding and performing makes it likely that you'll never deeply connect with anyone, because no one can see or be with who you really are. Like a rat in a maze, you can travel this same path in relationship after relationship and, after many years of this, see the pattern as irrefutable proof that you are indeed unlovable.

In this way, once you take on an identity of deficiency, your thoughts and interpretations can fuel the suffering associated with feeling unworthy. Emotions become the flames that roar from thoughts of being deficient and give rise to perceptions and actions that can define your life. In a sense, your life provides the vehicle for your expectations, and it takes you just where you think you'll go. If your life vehicle were a hot air balloon, you could inject thoughts about your inadequacy into the emotional blast furnace, which would pump out the searing heat of shame, expanding and inflating the balloon of your damaged ego. A sense of self as separate from everyone else takes flight. As long as you use these thoughts to fuel the furnace, you'll continue to feed the flames of suffering. Your damaged sense of self will rise higher and higher into winds that carry you into the same disaster again and again until you know beyond a shadow of a doubt that there's something terribly wrong with you. In the case of those who struggle with a sense of unworthiness, Descartes's dictum would be "I think, therefore I suffer."

The Price of Avoidance

We've explored how we get lost in thoughts and emotions by being overcome or identified with them, but one of the most onerous ways to create suffering is to stuff thoughts and emotions into the unconscious. In the language of psychology, this is an ego defense mechanism known as *repression*, which means "to make unconscious." Both thoughts and feelings can become poisonous if you stuff them into dark, unexplored recesses of the mind, but most often it's disturbing emotions that we try to banish. They may disappear from your conscious awareness, but they don't disappear from your unconscious attitude toward life, and they therefore remain available to serve as the basis of a sense of unworthiness or inadequacy.

To heal this suffering, you must find a way to investigate these dark, shadowy places and then gradually reintegrate banished thoughts and feelings back into your personality. In 12-step groups, it's said that "you're only as sick as your secrets." This speaks to the value of telling your truth and confessing your secrets—to yourself at a minimum, and to at least one other person if you can.

Much of psychotherapy is built upon the understanding that repression is a primary cause of psychopathology (a word that literally means "suffering of the soul"). Depression, anxiety, phobia, addiction, and many other psychological problems can be attempts to avoid painful and unwanted thoughts and feelings. For example, depression is often regarded as a substitute for more painful feelings, such as anger. It's sometimes said that depression is anger turned inward. As awful as depression or other forms of psychopathology can feel, we may prefer them to the feelings of shame, horror, or terror that they obscure.

Exploring the Shadows

To heal the inadequate and unworthy self, you'll have to find the things you've rejected and stuffed into the shadows. Both psychotherapy and meditation help make the unconscious conscious, bringing the light of awareness and compassion into the dark and hidden places of the mind and heart. You can learn to peer into your own shadow and stay with sources of shame and inadequacy with self-compassion and acceptance. In time, you can learn to embrace parts of yourself long disowned because they seemed too awful or painful to accept. Of course, this is difficult work, but it's crucial if you are to lay down the burden of feelings like shame, inadequacy, and unworthiness. You don't even have to go searching for these repressed inner experiences by means of meditation or therapy. If you give them a little space, awareness, and receptivity, the things you've been avoiding will surface on their own.

Keep in mind that emotions, including feelings like shame and self-blame, don't go away when you repress them. They're just relegated to the unconscious—your shadow—where they fester, become toxic, and create psychological problems and even physical illness. This can be a downward spiral, as these problems serve to further distract you from feeling the feelings you need to feel.

The only way to free yourself from these disorders of mind and body is to address the root cause: the feelings you've been trying to avoid. The path of healing involves feeling these blocked and rejected emotions, acknowledging them, and learning to stay with them and let them be. In time, you'll learn to follow your heart and come to terms with things the way they are, including difficult inner experiences like thoughts and emotions.

Attending to Thoughts and Emotions

We humans tend to identify with so many things: our name, our profession, our possessions, what we've done, where we've been, what's happened to us, and the list goes on. It's important to remember that all of these perspectives view the self as a thing in relation to many other things but neglect the most important perspective of all: that you exist only in this moment.

We've been looking at the ways an inadequate self can be created so that you can come to understand this self and its origins. It's helpful to have some understanding of why you are the way you are, but it's even more helpful to see what you're doing now, in each successive moment of your life. This is the mental faculty that will allow you to observe the mental loom on which you are weaving your life right now. This awareness is the light that can illuminate and dispel the stories you repeat to yourself that make you feel unworthy. This is essential if you are to dis-identify from this narrative-based self and realize the peace and happiness that has always been within you. Sometimes we can only recognize who we really are when we can take note of who we are not.

Mindfulness Practice: Noting

This time-honored practice will help you develop skill in recognizing and acknowledging what's happening in your body and mind as you meditate. The key is to make your acknowledgments extremely brief so you don't get caught in the thinking process of analyzing mental or physical activity. As soon as you note what you experience, acknowledge it and return to mindfulness of the breath.

This is a practice you can use anytime you're meditating, particularly when you notice that the mind is quite active. Sometimes you'll notice thoughts and feelings about what you like or don't like, or want or don't want. Just acknowledge them with the word "judging." At other times you may have feelings of attachment, in which case you can acknowledge "clinging." Other thoughts and emotions will bring up aversion, in which case you might acknowledge "repulsion" or "aversion." Let these internal experiences come and go as they will, and let all of it be. In the moments when you witness and note judgments, desires, and aversions and allow them to come and go, you aren't controlled by them and they cannot spin the spell of unworthiness. In this way, noting gives you a little distance from unwholesome mental states, which will help you free yourself from them.

The intention of this practice is not to actively search for mental states but to sit quietly and observe whatever arises. If nothing arises, simply be with the breath as an anchor to the present moment. Give yourself about thirty minutes for this practice. Choose a place to sit where you feel safe and at ease and won't be disturbed. Turn off your phone and other electronic devices. It may help to inform your family or friends that you are meditating or to put a "Do Not Disturb" sign on your door.

> Sit comfortably and settle into mindfulness of the breath until you feel fully present, letting your breath come and go normally and naturally.
>
> Staying in touch with the breath, expand your awareness to observe your physical state. Note sensations as they arise and

fall away, and acknowledge them with a simple phrase, such as "aching back" or "tight jaw." If a sensation is extremely unpleasant, shift your posture if that will help; otherwise simply note physical sensations, letting them be and staying centered with the breath. Stay with awareness of physical states for about five minutes.

Still staying in touch with the breath, turn your attention to thoughts, simply noting thoughts and letting them be. The acknowledgment may be as simple as "thinking," if you like, or you may note something more specific, such as "planning" or "worrying." Keep it simple. The more complicated and analytical you become, the more likely you are to get enmeshed in thinking. Stay with awareness of thoughts for about five minutes.

Still staying in touch with the breath, turn your attention to emotions, simply noting emotions and letting them be. Again, keep it simple. You may choose to use very broad acknowledgments, such as "pleasant," "unpleasant," or "neutral," or you can be more specific, with labels such as "sadness" or "peace." Stay with awareness of emotions for about five minutes.

Conclude by returning to the breath and practicing mindfulness of the breath for ten minutes.

Take some time to write in your journal about what you experienced in this meditation. List the words you used to note what you witnessed in this practice, and write about how this "one step removed" way of witnessing mental and emotional states influenced your reactions to specific thoughts and emotions. As you practiced, did you have any thoughts that usually sweep you into turmoil? Did noting them change your typical reaction to those thoughts?

As you become more adept at noting, it will become more effortless. With time, this practice will help you come to recognize that sensations, thoughts, and emotions are impermanent. They come and they go, and they are not you. Like all other skills, noting grows with practice, so continue to work with it both formally and informally. It can be a powerful tool in defusing destructive mental habits.

Savoring This Journey

In this chapter you learned another foundational mindfulness practice: noting. Actively observing and acknowledging your experience, including mental and emotional states, offers the liberating insight that you are not your thoughts or emotions, and that you can witness these ephemeral, moment-to-moment experiences from the far more expansive orientation of mindfulness. We encourage you to practice noting frequently for the next several weeks. Once you've practiced noting formally for a while, it will become a more natural, ingrained way of looking at and relating to your world—and a way of not taking yourself and judgments about yourself so seriously.

Chapter 3

~

Creating a Mindfulness Practice

What can anyone give you greater than now,
starting here, right in this room, when you turn around?

—William Stafford

In chapter 1, we discussed how a sense of inadequacy develops from a Western psychological perspective; we also explored the Buddhist perspective, which regards all notions of a separate self as fallacy. Chapter 2 looked at the nature of thoughts and emotions and how they can feed a sense of being deficient. In this chapter we'll start to take a closer look at mindfulness and how to apply it to your situation. We consider mindfulness to be foundational in working with feelings of unworthiness and transforming them. It will bring the light of awareness into the dark and unacknowledged places of your psyche to help dissolve self-limiting stories about who are so that you can begin to experience more self-compassion and freedom.

What Is Mindfulness?

Mindfulness is an ancient practice that, in essence, involves being an objective and nonjudgmental observer of whatever arises in the present moment. Buddhist monk and scholar Bhikkhu Analayo, who wrote a translation and commentary on the four foundations of mindfulness, says, "The purpose of *sati* [mindfulness] is solely to make things conscious, not to eliminate them" (Analayo 2003, 58). Because mindfulness meditation is centered on understanding the roots of suffering and experiencing greater freedom, it's considered a form of insight meditation (Buddhist practices for gaining insight into the nature of reality). The purpose isn't explicitly either relaxation or visualization.

The essence of mindfulness practice is deep inquiry into the workings of the mind to identify the causes of suffering and live with more peace and happiness. As you gain more understanding of what fuels your sense of inadequacy, shame, or unworthiness, you'll feel better. Succinctly put, mindfulness practice can help you experience freedom from all that enslaves you with clinging, aversion, and unawareness. It plays an extremely important role in mental development by giving you the ability to step back and watch the mind clearly, without distortions or misconceptions. It's like being a spectator at a play, objective and nonreactive, rather than being an actor, caught up in living out the plot. By observing yourself in this way, you can begin to recognize your old, habitual reactions and learn to respond to events with more skill and more ease.

These qualities of mindfulness highlight its value in alleviating feelings of deficiency or unworthiness. The ancient Buddhist text the Dhammapada says, "Mind is the forerunner of all...conditions. Mind is chief; and they are mind-made" (Narada Thera 2004, p. 1). Therefore, Buddhist psychology emphasizes the importance of intention or volition, since these are considered to be the seed of all endeavors, shaping all of your thoughts, words, and actions. If your intentions are kind, the results will be beneficial. Conversely, if they're unkind, the results will be nonbeneficial. From this point of view, you are the architect of your own heaven and hell by means of your own intentions. This is good news, because it means that you possess great potential for positive change. Mindfulness can play a significant role in your psychological and physical well-being by helping you see "under the hood" of the unconscious patterns that drive your behaviors—a necessary first step in making changes.

Mindfulness as a Way of Life

Mindfulness is a way of learning how to relate directly to your life, rather than to the preconceptions you have about life. No one else can do this work for you. As an old saying in mindfulness meditation circles puts it, "You cannot breathe out of my nostrils, and I cannot breathe out of yours."

You may wonder if you're capable of doing this work. Rest assured that you can. Mindfulness isn't something that you have to "get" or even learn, for it's already within you. It's just a matter of accessing it by becoming present. Here's a simple but profound truth: The moment you realize you aren't present, you're present once again. So you can become mindful again and again. Mindfulness is always that close.

In a larger sense, mindfulness is a way of life that you can manifest in two ways: through formal practice and through informal practice. Formal practice means taking time out each day for a specific period to intentionally sit, lie, or even stand and do certain forms of meditation. We'll introduce several formal practices in this book, including mindful breathing, the body scan, mindfulness meditation, and loving-kindness meditation. We encourage you to do some sort of formal practice for forty-five minutes daily, but if you can't manage that much time, thirty or fifteen minutes is fine. Indeed, even a minute of mindfulness can be beneficial. Do the best you can, and however long you practice, consider it an incredible gift that you are giving yourself—and something that no one else can give you.

Informal mindfulness practices involve bringing mindful awareness into your day-to-day life and activities—simply being mindful of daily tasks and experiences. We've all heard the advice to take life one day at a time. Mindfulness means taking life *one moment* at a time. And after all, since you really live only in the present moment, why not be there for it fully? You can be mindful as you're brushing your teeth, washing the dishes, walking, working, talking, eating, folding laundry, spending time with family or friends—anything and everything that you do.

Now you may be getting worried that you'll have a hard time being mindful in your day-to-day life. Such difficulties are inevitable, and not another reason to judge yourself as inadequate or lacking. Know that this happens to everyone, even the most experienced practitioners of mindfulness meditation. The key is to practice with kindness and, when you realize that you haven't been present, acknowledge that there's nothing you can do about what has already happened. Instead, simply start again, in that moment, and be present and open to all possibilities.

Edward Espe Brown, Zen priest and author, says it simply in his poem "No Measuring Up" (2009, 332):

Now I take the time
to peel potatoes, wash lettuce,
and boil beets, to scrub floors,
clean sinks, and empty trash.
Absorbed in the everyday,
I find time to unbind, unwind,
to invite the whole body, mind,
breath, thought, and wild impulse
to join, to bask in the task.
No time lost thinking
that somewhere else is better.
No time lost imagining
getting more elsewhere.
No way to tell this moment
does not measure up.
Hand me the spatula:
now is the time to taste what is.

There's an all-too-human tendency to get lost in thoughts about the past or the future. And even if these thoughts are positive, when we're busy thinking about the past or future, we're missing life itself. Perhaps you've noticed that you aren't very present in your moment-to-moment life. Maybe you're rehearsing what you're planning to do in the hopes that it will help you come off better and feel more worthy, or perhaps you're rehashing what you've done and thinking about how you could have done it better. Either way, you're missing whatever is happening right now.

As you become more mindful and allow yourself to be fully in the present, you'll gradually enlarge your experience of life and learn to be with yourself with curiosity and compassion, acknowledging and embracing all aspects of yourself and your experience—the good, the bad, and the ugly, in your physical sensations, thoughts, and emotions. You'll also gradually enlarge that critical space between the stimulus and the response, allowing you to choose your response, rather than reacting habitually.

Mindfulness gives you more options about how to act when you feel triggered, allowing you to respond, rather than react, to feelings of deficiency. When you react to stress, you fall into old, unconscious knee-jerk reactions. When you respond, you're mindful that you're experiencing stress and see that you have the option to do something more constructive. This allows you to escape the trap of habitual patterns that continue to foster feelings of shame or unworthiness.

Practicing Mindfulness

Practicing mindfulness is being here and now on purpose, without striving and without judging. Being here for this moment reveals how precious it is, if for no other reason than because each moment that passes will never return again. This moment, and this moment, and this moment—this is where you live…or not. We usually don't use the phrase "having the time of my life" other than when things are going great, but in truth, each moment actually is the time of your life. You may judge it as positive or negative, pleasant or unpleasant, but the fact is, this moment is all you really have.

Mindfulness Practice: Cultivating Spaciousness

Realize that, in cultivating mindfulness, you're giving a gift of love to yourself. To support your practice and the time and intentions you invest in it, give yourself another gift: a space dedicated to your practice. Find a place in your home to create a quiet and uncluttered space, free from the distractions that might draw you outside of yourself—the sounds, the devices, the many things that so often seem to beg to be dealt with. As you make this physical space for yourself, reflect on how sitting in meditation is a way of clearing a space in your mind and sitting within it. This is what enables you to witness whatever enters that space in each moment. Once you've cleared a physical space for yourself, the following practice will help you clear some space in your mind. Give yourself about twenty minutes for this practice.

Begin by bringing awareness to your breath, using the felt sense of your breath coming and going from your belly or nostrils as your way to be present. Let your breath flow naturally as you practice mindful breathing for ten minutes.

Now notice how thoughts, like the sensations of breathing, are also coming and going, and that you may get drawn into them, or you may not. Mindful awareness is the mental space in which you can recognize sensations, thoughts, and emotions coming and going. It's the sky, and the mental and physical events occurring within you are clouds that appear, evolve, and disappear. You don't need to do anything with these passing events. Just observe as they come and go. If you get drawn into any of these passing events, notice this too, then let it be and return your attention to the wide-open sky of awareness. Being present...

Sit within this space of awareness for ten minutes, or longer if you like. When you're ready, thank yourself for this gift of mindfulness practice, and for creating this calm, open space where you can simply be and observe.

Take some time to write in your journal about what you discovered here. What was it like to be the open sky of awareness and let the weather systems of the body and mind come and go? Did you notice and experience how even feelings of shame or inadequacy are ever-changing and impermanent?

Having a quiet, uncluttered place to practice is helpful. However, you can sit in this kind of wide-open awareness anywhere and witness the rising and falling of sensations, thoughts, and emotions. In this internal space, you can see that all of these phenomena are impermanent, including your stories, your problems, and all the things you fear, cling to, long for, or regret. Notice how the whole parade can just pass though this space and you can witness it without joining it. This is how you transcend the identity of unworthiness that you've authored through your long history with yourself. This is where you can notice, and become, something new.

~ Joe's Story

Joe, a middle-aged plumber, frequently lost his temper while working and had alienated many customers as a result. When former customers didn't seek his services again, he found himself depressed and self-blaming: "If only I was more patient! If only I could keep my mouth shut! I'm so frigging stupid!" He had been down this path many, many times, and over the years had created a well-worn groove of self-judgment, blame, and pain. After years of treading this same path and getting nowhere other than deeper in self-loathing, Joe realized that something needed to change. A friend recommended a mindfulness-based stress reduction (MBSR) program, and Joe somewhat reluctantly decided to give it a try. Before long, he was sold on the approach, as mindfulness helped him learn to recognize those familiar angry surges and the impulses to strike out and react.

As Joe practiced staying with and acknowledging those feelings, he began to notice that he did indeed have a choice, that he could respond more skillfully to frustrations. He also became mindful of how he held his body when he was angry and realized that he had a lot of muscular tension. He saw that he had a choice here, too—that he could release much of that tension, and that when he did, he felt better physically.

As his practice deepened, Joe began to understand what was fueling his impatience and frustration. As he sat with and explored his anger, he remembered old feelings of never being able to do anything good or worthy in his dad's eyes, and how this had made him feel he was irredeemably inadequate. As the weight of not being good enough began to fade, Joe found he had more patience. This gave him the space to respond to stressful situations mindfully and helped him tolerate frustrations and setbacks. He knew he still had a long way to go, but he had the distinct feeling that he was on the right track.

The Attitudinal Foundations of Mindfulness

Up to this point we've offered you short meditation practices focusing on the breath and on noting physical sensations, thoughts, and emotions. Shortly, we'll present the body scan, a longer formal practice. As you begin to deepen your practice with the body scan, it's important to cultivate certain qualities that are essential to mindfulness meditation. The eight attitudes described below are some important foundations of mindfulness. They provide a way to hold, investigate, and work with whatever comes up in your practice, and in your life. Cultivating them will deepen your mindfulness. And although they're crucial for anyone, they also have a bearing on freeing yourself from feelings of being flawed or unworthy, as we'll discuss below.

Beginner's mind. This is a frame of mind that sees moment-to-moment experience in a new way. In regard to feeling deficient, it opens the door to seeing yourself differently, rather than remaining trapped in the narrative-based self. This frees you to step out of old, conditioned ways of relating to yourself and to others.

Nonjudgment. This attitude brings a sense of impartiality and openness to any experience, including your experience of yourself. By practicing nonjudgment you can begin to free yourself from feeling less than (or more than) others. Nonjudgment helps you see that we're all trying to live our lives the best we can, and that each of us has been wounded and has also hurt others, usually due to unawareness and fear.

Nonstriving. This quality allows you to be where you are. Many people spend so much of life either seeking certain experiences or avoiding them—both ways of getting away from what's right here. Nonstriving can help release you from the pangs of wanting to be somehow different and allow you to be who you are with an open and curious heart.

Acknowledgment. To acknowledge is to validate your direct experience. The gateway into healing the unworthy self lies in the ability to observe and acknowledge things as they are.

Letting be. Letting be is a balanced state of mind that allows things to be as they are. It's a precursor to letting go of things that don't serve your well-being. As you begin to acknowledge whatever you're feeling, you'll find that the way through it is to ride the waves of what is.

Self-reliance. Self-reliance means trusting your own direct experience in the moment. As you grow in self-reliance, you'll grow in self-confidence, which will help you free yourself from limited and limiting definitions of yourself.

Self-compassion. This is the greatest elixir for a heart that has hardened against itself. Self-compassion is about opening to yourself with kindness and tenderness, rather than self-blame and criticism.

Equanimity. This quality of awareness is the ability to be with things as they are with emotional balance and wisdom. It involves understanding and accepting the inevitability of change and seeing through the misconception of a fixed notion of self. This can free you from identification with shame, inadequacy, and unworthiness.

One of the things you may recognize with these qualities of mind is that they actually characterize the mental faculty of awareness, which all human beings possess but often neglect. Cultivating these qualities of mind will nourish your practice and your life.

Working with Challenges

It is absolutely normal to experience some challenges when practicing mindfulness meditation. Your mind will wander; this happens to everyone. Since you've begun practicing mindfulness with the approaches earlier in the book, there's no doubt that you've already experienced this. Your mind can be just like the weather often is—changing all the time. You've probably noticed that you tend to get lost in memories or thoughts about the future, even in everyday life. For example, when eating breakfast you might be planning the day ahead or remembering the past, whether marveling at how wonderful last weekend was or how painful that interaction was that you had with your spouse last night. It seems that most of our waking hours are spent thinking about the past or the future, and that we seldom live in the here and now. As you look closely at the workings of your mind during mindfulness practice, you'll start to see how often you aren't present.

Your job isn't to berate yourself for this, but to simply acknowledge the wandering and come back to the meditation. If you find it difficult to resist criticizing yourself, consider this: If you weren't mindful, you wouldn't even know you'd wandered off. What's important is that you came back to the present moment.

Working with the wandering mind offers three benefits. The first is that every time you bring the mind back from wandering, you're building the muscle of concentration. It actually is like lifting weights. The mind wanders off and you bring it back again and again. Through repetition you build muscle mass—and concentration. The second benefit is that when you come back into the present moment and notice where you drifted off to, you can discover elements of doubt, desire, or anger that you were caught up in. This offers insight into hindrances and difficulties, including how the judgmental mind creates feelings of deficiency and inadequacy. You may also become aware of worry, sadness, or confusion, perhaps signaling that you need to pay closer attention to or deal with certain things in your life. The third benefit is that you gain an understanding of the mind-body connection and how the thoughts you think and emotions you feel have a physical reflection in the body. You begin to understand how a tight jaw or upset stomach, for example, is the expression of certain thoughts and emotions in your body.

Other challenges show up in the form of the five hindrances: desire, anger, restlessness, sleepiness, and doubt. These problems are so common, predictable, and prevalent in mindfulness practice that many books on mindfulness meditation address how to work with them.

~ Desire, or the craving mind, is an aspect of mind that's preoccupied with things like wanting to feel good. It spends a lot of time in fantasies, daydreams, and plans. When you feel unworthy, you may be consumed with the desire to be better or different. It's like a thirst or hunger that seldom lets up.

~ Anger reflects not being okay with the way things are. You may feel mad at yourself for being so inadequate. The angry mind becomes engrossed in aversion, resentment, or hatred.

~ Restlessness is like a pacing tiger. When your mind is filled with shame, it becomes unsettled and seethes with unharnessed energy that's uncomfortable to sit with and stay with. It can make you feel like you want to crawl out of your skin, like you need to do something or go somewhere else.

~ With sleepiness, your concentration will be dull and you'll feel listless or tired or have low energy. Unworthiness, shame, or inadequacy may feel so overwhelming that you just want to collapse, disappear, not be here, and go to sleep.

~ With doubt, you may wonder if meditation serves any purpose or can help you in any way. You may become filled with self-doubt and believe that it isn't possible to heal and be okay with who you are. This makes it all the easier to fall into the other four hindrances.

All five hindrances are challenging and can get in the way of your practice. That's why it's so important to notice when they're occurring and to be able to name and acknowledge them. As you learned in regard to the practice of noting, naming in and of itself helps create some distance, and this will help loosen the grip of the five hindrances. The moment you realize you're trapped, you've become mindful and can begin to step out of the trap.

Sometimes the metaphor of a clear pond is helpful in understanding how to work with the hindrances, as each hindrance obscures your ability to clearly see the beautiful pebbles at the bottom of the pond. When you're in a state of desire, the pond doesn't appear clear; it's colored with the red dye of passion. Your desires color everything. Try to stay still and breathe mindfully to calm your body and mind. If you're angry, the water freezes over and becomes hardened with ice, and this too obscures your view. Maybe this is a signal to open to the warmth of compassion. With restlessness, the waters are choppy. Begin to harness that energy in a constructive way, rather than letting it bite you in the butt. If you're sleepy, the waters are covered with algae. Perhaps it's best to wake up and recognize that you aren't going to be here forever. With doubt, the pond appears cloudy or muddy. This is a signal to reflect on why you're doing this practice and what you've learned about yourself so far. May this give you incentive to persevere.

When you become mindful that any of the hindrances are present, notice how your body and mind feel. Sense the texture of these states and notice what happens when you become entranced by them. Are you more at ease with yourself or less?

Mindfulness Practice: The Body Scan

The body scan is a powerful formal mindfulness practice that will help you reconnect with your body and your mind. Both of us have taught numerous classes on mindfulness, and we can't tell you how many times we've heard people say they have virtually no awareness of their body, almost as if the body didn't exist. As you practice the body scan, you'll come into contact with more than just your body; you'll directly contact your life. Your body is the vehicle you live inside of as you travel through this life, and your entire life history resides within it: all of your thoughts, emotions, dreams, and memories, all of your experiences. When working with feelings of unworthiness or inadequacy, the body scan can be a tremendous resource. It will help you to recognize what you are feeling physically and how these sensations are connected to your history and the stories with which you construct an identity of unworthiness.

The body scan is a methodical practice that begins with awareness of your left foot and systematically proceeds through the entire body, part by part, up to your head. As you focus on each part, you attend to the felt sense of that part of your body. How is it feeling? Are any sensations present? Are they pleasant, unpleasant, or neutral? You're like a scientist, feeling and observing your direct, moment-to-moment experience; itches, aches, tingles, warmth, coolness—whatever. In addition to physical sensations, you also aim to become mindful of and acknowledge any thoughts or emotions evoked by the practice.

Do this practice in a relaxing environment without distractions. We suggest lying down while doing the body scan, but if you find yourself sleepy or would rather sit or stand, you are welcome to do so. Whatever your position, bring your full, undivided attention to this practice. Read through the entire exercise before you begin the practice. If possible, give yourself at least thirty minutes for this practice. When focusing on specific parts of the body, try to spend a minute or two with each part, though if you're short on time you can certainly do less. Initially you may find it helpful to record the instructions and listen to the recording as you practice. If you do, remember to include a pause before shifting to each new part of the body. You can also purchase a CD of the body scan at www.yourheartwideopen.com. Soon enough you'll be familiar with the practice and won't need to listen to the instructions. We've adapted the instructions below from *A Mindfulness-Based Stress Reduction Workbook*, by Bob Stahl and Elisha Goldstein (New Harbinger Publications, 2010).

Take a few moments to welcome yourself to the spacious mindfulness in which you'll practice the body scan.

Begin by doing a mindful check-in, feeling into your physical sensations, thoughts, and emotions. Whatever you find, just let it be. Perhaps it's been a busy day and this is the first time you're slowing down. Allow yourself to simply feel how you are and what you're carrying with you into this meditation, and let it be. There's no need to judge, analyze, or figure things out. Just acknowledge how you're feeling. Spend about two minutes with the mindful check-in.

Now gently shift your focus to the breath. Bring your attention to either the nose, the chest, or the abdomen—wherever you feel the breath most prominently and distinctly. Just be mindful of breathing in and out. Breathing in and knowing you're breathing in... Breathing out and knowing you're breathing out...

At times you may notice that your mind wanders away from the breath. When you recognize this, acknowledge wherever you went to and then come back to your breath, breathing in and out with awareness. Spend about two minutes with awareness of the breath.

Now gently shift your focus from breathing to the body scan. Begin by bringing your attention to the felt sense of your entire body: how it is feeling and any sensations that you're experiencing. Throughout this practice, you may come across areas that are tight or tense. If so, just let the sensations be, giving them space to go wherever they need to go. If any thoughts or emotions arise, just let them be as well. Allow yourself to simply acknowledge whatever is present in body and mind and let it be.

Now bring your awareness to the bottom of the left foot, wherever you feel the foot contacting the floor. It could be the back of the heel or the bottom of the foot.

Expand your awareness to feel into the entire left foot, feeling into the heel, ball, and sole of the foot. Feel into the toes and the top of the foot.

Now shift your awareness back into the Achilles tendon and up into the left ankle.

Now shift your awareness up to the lower left leg, feeling into the calf and shin and the lower leg's connection to the knee.

Now let your awareness rise up to the left thigh, sensing into the upper leg and its connection into the left hip.

And now gently withdraw your awareness from the left hip down to the left foot and move to the right foot, bringing awareness to wherever you feel the foot contacting the floor. It could be the back of the heel or the bottom of the foot.

Expand your awareness to feel into the entire right foot, feeling into the heel, ball, and sole of the foot. Feel into the toes and the top of the foot.

Now shift your awareness back into the Achilles tendon and up into the right ankle.

Now shift your awareness up to the lower right leg, feeling into the calf and shin and the lower leg's connection to the knee.

Now let your awareness rise up into the right thigh, sensing into the upper leg and its connection into the right hip.

Now shift your awareness into the pelvic girdle, home to the systems of elimination, sexuality, and reproduction, feeling into the genitals, buttocks, and anal region. Be mindful of any sensations, thoughts, or emotions and just let them be.

Now shift your awareness to the belly and abdomen, home to the systems of digestion and assimilation. Feel into the belly and abdomen with awareness and let them be.

Now bring your awareness down into the tailbone and the base of the spine and begin to sense into the lower back, feeling any sensations and letting them be.

Now shift your awareness to the middle back, feeling any sensations and letting them be.

Now shift your awareness to the upper back, feeling any sensations and letting them be. Let any sensations go wherever they need to go, like ripples expanding outward. If you feel any tightness, pain, or discomfort and can soften those sensations, let that happen. If you cannot, just let them be.

Now gently shift your awareness into the chest, feeling into the skin of the chest, breasts, and rib cage, and deeper within to lungs and heart, home of respiration and circulation. Being present to any physical sensations, thoughts, or emotions and letting them be...

Now gently withdraw attention from the chest and shift to the fingertips of the left hand, feeling into the fingers and palm, and then the back of the hand and up into the left wrist.

Now shift your awareness to the left forearm and its connection into the elbow.

Now shift your awareness to the upper left arm and its connection into the shoulder and armpit, feeling the sensations in your upper arm and shoulder.

Now gently withdraw awareness from the left shoulder down to the left fingertips, then move to the fingertips of the right hand, feeling into the fingers and palm, and then the back of the hand and up into the right wrist.

Now shift your awareness to the right forearm and its connection into the elbow.

Now shift your awareness to the upper right arm and its connection into the right shoulder and armpit, feeling the sensations in your upper arm and shoulder.

Now bring your awareness into both shoulders, feeling any sensations and just letting them be.

Now bring your awareness up into the neck and throat, being present to any sensations, thoughts, or emotions and simply letting them be.

Let your awareness rise up into your jaw, teeth, tongue, mouth, and lips, feeling any sensations and allowing them to go wherever they need to go.

Expand your awareness into the cheeks, the forehead, and the temples, feeling into the eyes, the muscles around the eyes, and the sinus passages that go deep into the head. Being present…

Now feel into the top and back of the head, into the ears, and then inside the head, into the brain. Feel into your face and head, home to your brain and the senses—the eyes that see, the nose that smells, the ears that hear, the tongue that tastes, the body that feels.

Now begin to expand your field of awareness to the entire body. Feel how the head is connected to the neck, shoulders, arms, hands, chest, back, belly, hips, pelvic region, legs, and feet. Feel your body from head to toes and fingertips as a whole organism. Being present…

Breathing in, feel the whole body rising and expanding as you inhale. Breathing out, feel the whole body descending and contracting as you exhale. Being present…

As you come to the end of the body scan, congratulate yourself for taking this time to be present.

Take some time to write in your journal about how the body scan went. What came up for you in your body, thoughts, and emotions? What did you discover? For example, did you feel any tension or tightness in any areas of your body? Did any of the sensations you experienced evoke any memories? Did any of them bring up feelings of unworthiness or inadequacy or, conversely, happiness or connectedness?

The body scan is a very concrete, noncomplex place to start the work of self-acceptance and nonjudging. When practicing the body scan, you may begin to see how your feelings of inadequacy, shame, or unworthiness are connected to your body and mind states. You may observe critical or self-loathing judgments that arise from your perceptions of your body image, or you may discover how you've stored bodily tension from past emotional wounds. All of this helps prepare you for applying mindfulness to phenomena that are more amorphous, such as thoughts and emotions, in a similar way.

Savoring This Journey

In this chapter we presented two new mindfulness practices: cultivating spaciousness and the body scan.

Cultivating spaciousness will help you develop the foundations of mindfulness, particularly nonjudging, nonstriving, acknowledgment, and letting be. It will also help you create some space so that you can witness your experience without becoming entangled in it. This will serve as an important orientation in all mindfulness practices you engage in. We recommend that you engage in this practice frequently until you begin to practice formal mindfulness meditation, which you'll learn in the next chapter.

Because the body scan is both more structured and a longer practice, it will help you strengthen your mindful focus. And because the body and emotions are so closely intertwined, this practice also offers insight into your emotional state. With time, you can learn to recognize the physical signs of difficult thoughts and emotions and use them as signals that it would be a good idea to bring mindful awareness to whatever is going on with you. We recommend that you practice the body scan frequently at first, and that you continue to practice it weekly in the years to come, as a way of staying in touch with your body, mind, and emotions.

Chapter 4

Looking Behind the Curtain of Self

Self is the only prison that can ever bind the soul.

—Henry Van Dyke

Mindfulness meditation is an investigative practice. You enter a space of awareness in which you can witness and examine the thoughts and emotions from which you fabricate a sense of self. And as you sit and experience thoughts coming and going, you can't help but wonder from time to time, "Who's thinking these thoughts? If I'm witnessing them, where are they coming from?" You may also wonder why so many of them are repetitive or just plain nuts. Yet even as you observe how often you get drawn into and replay shaming and self-blaming stories, you'll also come to see that your identification with these stories isn't compulsory—it's entirely optional. With practice, you can learn to be with your thoughts and feel your emotions without turning them into defining stories about yourself.

In this chapter we'll help you cultivate mindfulness skills that will allow you to witness the stories that create an identity of deficiency, and help you see that you are much more than any story, no matter how long-standing. When you can witness the workings of your mind with dispassionate awareness, it's a little like looking behind the curtain where the Wizard of Oz was creating all of his illusions. Once you see the supposedly mighty wizard of your own storyteller frantically pushing buttons and turning switches to maintain an illusion, it's hard to remain entranced by the story. As you've begun to learn, the point of view that observes and recognizes these mental processes is distinct from them and holds the key to a much larger experience of who you are. This key opens your heart to freedom, wisdom, and compassion.

Opening Your Heart

Mindfulness is both a practice and a state of mind, a path and a destination—or, perhaps more accurately, it's a path that is its own destination. The practice is deliberately paying attention, without judgment, to the moments of your life in an open and caring way that isn't driven by desires or aversions. This spacious and accepting kind of awareness is a mental faculty we all have access to, though we may not employ it often. Usually we find ourselves in this wide-open state of mind quite by accident and, for a few minutes, are filled with wonder at the ordinary yet extraordinary marvel of life unfolding around us. Suddenly there's vividness and clarity in what we are witnessing. Time seems to slow down, the urgency to be somewhere or someone else vanishes, and your heart opens wide. Practicing mindfulness will bring more of these moments into your life.

∼ Krista's Story

Krista, a working mom with two kids, had been practicing mindfulness for about six weeks. On a morning like many others, she was struggling to make breakfast and the kids' lunches, get the kids dressed, and coordinate the evening's events with her husband—not to mention getting herself ready for work. She called her five-year-old son down for breakfast, but he didn't respond. Finally, she looked out the front window and saw him standing in the rain, shaping his hair into a Mohawk and catching raindrops on his tongue. Momentarily overwhelmed with frustration at the delay and his obliviousness, she started to yell at him to get in the house instantly. But in that moment, she saw the sheer delight in her son's face and felt a resonating joy for the happiness she was witnessing. Her rush to get everything done vanished, and time seemed to stand still.

She picked up her two-year-old daughter and spent another minute just watching her son and enjoying a kind of delight she hadn't felt for a long time. The beauty and happiness of the experience colored the rest of her day. And that evening, for the first time in a long time, she didn't criticize herself for being an inadequate mother—even though she'd taken her son to school late and with wet clothes on.

The Awareness That Sees Self Is Free of Self

Years ago at an extended meditation retreat, a meditation teacher informed us that he wasn't interested in any of our stories. We were stunned and taken aback—until he went on to acknowledge the profound tenderness, woundedness, and pain that our stories hold but said that he wanted to help us explore possibilities that lay beyond these self-limiting definitions of ourselves. As we sat with these ideas for a while, it brought home how easy it is to identify with old stories we've fallen for again and again, only to find ourselves in the same swarms of mental and emotional hornets that have stung us so many times before. How many times do we have to get stung before we see that the story isn't who we are? This is where mindfulness and self-compassion can be so beneficial. They allow you to see and acknowledge the tenderness and pain in your story without falling under the delusion that the story defines who you are. It may be your story, but it isn't you.

A pervasive sense of unworthiness has core components of self-blame, self-consciousness, and resentment. These habits of mind are all connected and stem from habitual ways of looking at things. In each moment, you're creating your sense of self. Anytime you recognize this self-constructing activity, it can help free you a little more from the confines of the self you've created.

Exercise: AWARE

An effective way of working with self-stories is summed up in the acronym AWARE, which stands for allow, witness, acknowledge, release, and ease up.

Allow all of your thoughts and feelings to come and go as they will. This will help you soften your reactions to whatever comes up for you in the space of mindful awareness. Allowing is a kind and curious attitude that enables you to look more deeply into your stories and learn from them rather than becoming entranced by them or trying to block them, both of which will just leave you more stuck. By allowing your experience in this way, you can learn to accept all thoughts as vehicles for insight rather than as proof of anything, including any inherent unworthiness or inadequacy. Allowing enables you to recognize that a thought is just a thought, whether you like it or not.

Witness the narrative with which you construct your sense of self. Sometimes you're the one who has acted: "I did…" "I should have…" "I shouldn't have…" "I wish I could have…" Sometimes you're the one who has been acted upon: "Somebody did this or that to me." "Everyone ignored me." "People always…" "No one ever…" Either way, it drones on and on as long as you indulge it. From the perspective of mindful awareness, you can witness the habitual ways your mind creates the narrative-based self without identifying with them. Witnessing is curious and nonjudging. It doesn't cling to or avoid anything. With this tool you can look more deeply into even very painful events with your heart wide open. Just as an emergency room physician looks deep into a wound without flinching and finds the shard at its core, you may discover things you no longer need to carry or blame yourself for.

Acknowledge what you experience happening in stories you tell about yourself. Using the noting practice from chapter 2, note the physical sensations, thoughts, and emotions you experience as they come and go. Remember to use simple phrases to acknowledge your experience, such as "frightened," "rejected," "lonely," and so on. Is there a character you are attempting to create or assassinate? Notice any repetitive or habitual elements through which you create the narrative-based self. Is there a theme? Is the storyteller cruel or kind, brilliant or blind? Are there familiar judgments? Are there familiar longings? Acknowledge all that you notice.

Release the self-concepts that you've fabricated with these old stories and concepts. Disidentify from your habitual and familiar ways of thinking of yourself. Fame, shame, loss, gain, pleasure, and pain are all transient experiences, not attributes of self. When you use allowing, witnessing, and acknowledging to see the storyteller at work, you can finally stop identifying with the self created by your stories. You don't have to believe everything you think. Why stay in a prison of self when the door is wide open? Let everything go. Let everything be.

Ease up and emerge from this trance of unworthiness. When you're stuck in a self-concept of inadequacy and unworthiness, a great deal of your self-talk involves comments about how you're doing, looking, or performing, and so much of this internal dialogue calls forth comparisons to others and judgments about yourself. This is neither necessary nor skillful, and it's never any fun. Everything isn't about you. Plus, when you're caught up in thoughts about yourself, you're missing what's actually happening in each irreplaceable moment of your life.

Allowing, witnessing, acknowledging, releasing, and easing up are primary skills in meditation practice and will also serve you well in the unfolding moments of your life—at work, at home, with friends, and in everything you do, particularly when you notice that your self-talk has become critical and unkind. AWARE can become a way of life that helps you grow a little freer each time you practice it.

Turning Toward the Wounded Place

Rumi, a thirteenth century poet and Sufi mystic, had deep insight into how a faulty, damaging self-story is created and maintained. In his poem "Childhood Friends" (1995, 142), he speaks to the issues we've been discussing:

> Trust your wound to a teacher's surgery.
> Flies collect on a wound. They cover it,
> those flies of your self-protecting feelings,
> your love for what you think is yours.
> Let a teacher wave away the flies
> and put a plaster on the wound.
> Don't turn your head. Keep looking
> at the bandaged wound. That's where
> the light enters you.
> And don't believe for a moment
> that you're healing yourself.

The wounds from painful life events can help you open to insight and healing when you bring compassionate awareness to them. Don't avert your eyes from your pain. You can't erase what happened—what you did or didn't do, or what others did or didn't do. If you acknowledge and accept these wounds, rather than looking away from them, they will become the site of healing. When you allow them and let them be and know them deeply, these old wounds can lead you back to your heart. For example, if you've done something you regret, the pain of shame can remind you of the consequences of unskillful actions and strengthen your resolve to respond differently in similar situations. Even if you've been hurt through no fault of your own, this pain can guide you to be careful about how you relate to others so you don't hurt them in the same way. This is a good thing. Just like physical pain helps us be careful with our bodies, emotional pain helps us be careful with our actions. An emotional wound becomes beneficial when the memories within it help you learn how to live your life more skillfully, with awareness and compassion.

Mindfulness Practice: Mindful Self-Inquiry

We can learn to be suspicious of particular thoughts, such as most judgmental and repetitive thoughts and any self-hating thoughts. There's wisdom in suspecting that something is amiss in this kind of thinking. It can lead to investigations and discoveries about how you color your world and how you make yourself miserable or happy through the filter of your thoughts. This type of investigation can help you see what is real and what isn't, and what thoughts to believe or not. When you don't automatically believe all of your thoughts, they'll lose their power to shape a faulty sense of self.

Mindful self-inquiry is a practice that can help you investigate anything, including the pain of old wounds, as well as other unpleasant thoughts and stories that create suffering. Because unworthiness is a kind of trance that obstructs clear seeing, self-inquiry can be useful in drawing back the veil and seeing the unconscious reactions that perpetuate the cycle of pain and suffering. It involves looking deeply and unflinchingly into your wounded heart in order to see things more objectively—without judgment and without avoidance. This work involves tenderness and a friendly kind of curiosity.

Give yourself at least thirty minutes for this practice. This work is difficult and may even feel threatening at times, so practice in a place that feels safe and where you can sit comfortably without being disturbed. If you like, gather a few objects that bring you comfort or that you treasure and set them on a shelf or table nearby.

Begin by practicing mindful breathing for at least ten minutes. Let your breath come and go as it will and use the sensations of breathing as your way to be present.

Take a few moments to reflect upon your life experience, with its ups and downs and the thread of shame or unworthiness that brought you to this book.

Now recall your earliest memories of feeling unworthy. Feel into any physical sensations these memories evoke, and be mindful of the emotions that arise and any limiting self-definitions that come up. Even if a memory is unpleasant, bring your curiosity and compassion to it, just like you might rest at the edge of a yoga stretch and breathe into the place of discomfort. Don't try to push through or escape from the memory and any discomfort associated with it; just be with your pain and woundedness with as much kindness and acceptance as possible.

Notice if this memory brings up any judgmental stories about you or your traits. If it does, acknowledge them, let them be, and then, as a way of grounding yourself in the present moment, direct your attention to whatever physical sensations you may be experiencing. Notice that as you attend to the immediacy of sensations, they are in the foreground of your consciousness and the thoughts and emotions of your narrative-based self are in the background. Continue with this practice for about ten minutes, reorienting to physical sensations anytime you begin to get lost in thoughts or emotions that define you as unworthy. Throughout this practice, notice if your feelings of unworthiness change in any way when you examine old stories while remaining in touch with the sensations of here and now.

Take a few minutes to return to mindfulness of the breath, then conclude this practice by reflecting on the courage that enabled you to explore these mental, emotional, and physical states. Congratulate yourself for being willing to take on this difficult work.

Take a little time to write in your journal about what came up for you physically, mentally, and emotionally as you practiced mindful self-inquiry. Describe any physical sensations that attended memories of feeling unworthy or inadequate, and any emotional experiences that came up for you in the process.

Know that to name a thing is to separate from it and is the first step in disidentifying from it. As you shift from difficult thoughts and emotions to physical sensations, you're reorienting from the narrative-based self to the immediacy-based self. As you continue to work with this practice, notice that the part of you that is aware of the memories, thoughts, emotions, and physical sensations related to feeling inadequate is one step removed from feelings of inadequacy. Your mindful, immediacy-based self is the one noticing the self-blaming and self-judging and the urges to hide or escape.

Mindful self-inquiry is a practice you can use for the rest of your life to investigate the stories and judgments you're telling yourself about yourself. It will help you discover the origins of these stories and how you get stuck in them. It opens the door to a way of being in the world that isn't confined by the narrative-based self. From this expanded awareness you can notice something new—a self that isn't imprisoned in a story, a self that exists and responds in the here and now, along with everyone and everything around you.

Bringing Light into the Darkness

As you practice mindful self-inquiry, you'll get increasingly in touch with what's going on inside you—the myriad thoughts and emotions sometimes referred to as the ten thousand joys and sorrows. Mindfulness provides a space for direct observation of all of these experiences without getting caught in the extremes of repression or entanglement, both of which can perpetuate as sense of unworthiness. You can learn to shift from your old ways of seeing to new possibilities.

We want to acknowledge that it can be enormously challenging to be an impartial observer when you're situated face-to-face with yourself in a hall of mirrors reflecting the emotions, thoughts, and memories underlying your feelings of shame, guilt, inadequacy, and a host of other unpleasant visitors. The gift of mindfulness is that it gives you room to observe this entourage of aversions, fantasies, judgments, and perceived slights as they come and go. Gradually, you'll learn to acknowledge these feelings and see more clearly into their origins and how they feed self-limiting definitions of who you are and who you can be. This will allow you to experience deeper states of acceptance, freedom, and peace.

As you embark on this difficult work, take solace in the advice of François Fénelon, a seventeenth-century Catholic priest, who spoke to this difficulty in a letter to a struggling parishioner (2002, 29):

> As that light increases, we see ourselves to be worse than we thought. We are amazed at our former blindness as we see issuing forth from the depths of our heart a whole swarm of shameful feelings, like filthy reptiles crawling from a hidden cave. We never could have believed that we had harbored such things, and we stand aghast as we watch them gradually appear… But while our faults diminish, the light by which we see them waxes brighter, and we are filled with horror. Bear in mind, for your comfort, that we only perceive our malady when the cure begins.

~ Henry's Story

When Henry was ten years old, his father had an affair with the woman next door, who had been his mom's best friend. One day they were discovered, and the next year was a catastrophe of endless battles. Henry's home was shattered. His parents divorced when he was twelve, and he and his mom moved into an apartment with strange furniture and noisy neighbors.

Henry knew his dad had done something bad, but he continued loving him in spite of that. He could visit his dad just once a week, and those visits usually felt weird because his dad was drinking a lot and grumpy and said such mean things about his mom. Though his dad had a swimming pool, Henry was ashamed to bring his friends over because his dad was unpredictable and embarrassed him by monopolizing their attention with drunken warnings about the untrustworthiness of women and the world in general.

Meanwhile, his mom made new friends and joined a church, and although she seemed happier, she had changed. She started talking about God a lot and eventually married a man who was nice, but who also talked about God a lot. Henry wanted his old mom back. He felt like he'd lost both his mother and his father. It seemed like they didn't love him anymore, and he wondered if it was his fault.

Years later, in high school, a girl Henry loved dumped him because he was flirting with another girl. Before long, his girlfriend was going steady with someone else. Everyone knew what had happened, and Henry felt ashamed. To him, it seemed he had made the same mistake his father had, and he took it as proof he was faulty and unworthy. Little by little, new embarrassments and failures made him feel even worse about himself, and by the time he was a senior he was using drugs and skipping school. He told himself that it didn't matter what anyone thought about him; he was damaged goods anyway.

Healthy Shame vs. Toxic Shame

In his best-selling book *Healing the Shame That Binds You* (1988), John Bradshaw makes a distinction between healthy shame and toxic shame. In doing so, he helped the Western world see a truth long known in the ancient psychology of Buddhism: Healthy shame is a signal that you've done something wrong, whereas toxic shame says that you *are* something wrong. Healthy shame refers to specific events, whereas toxic shame becomes your identity (Bradshaw 1988). Healthy shame is a good thing. It's a part of your moral compass and helps guide you to make choices that don't injure others. Toxic shame, on the other hand, is a creation of the narrative-based self and seems to define who you are. It begins to poison you as you identify with the negative judgments you tell yourself or hear from others.

Shame and Dread as Guardians of the World

In Buddhist psychology, what John Bradshaw calls healthy shame is united with moral dread to create twin emotions that are considered the guardians of the world. Moral dread is the anxious feeling that arises when you're about to do something similar to actions that created shame in your past. If you grow numb to these guardians, you're in peril. Without shame and dread to guide your actions, you can do things that hurt others and yourself.

Repressing healthy shame because it feels bad would be like removing smoke alarms from your house because you can't stand their ear-piercing sound. When the warnings of your moral guidance system go unheard, you can end up burning in the flames of disastrous choices.

That said, even healthy shame is very painful and can be searing in its own right. Yet there's a reason for this. The brain is designed to function like Velcro for negative events and Teflon for positive events (R. Siegel 2010). This isn't a cruel stroke of fate. There's actually an evolutionary value to this bias of memory: Having a better memory of negative events helps us avoid them in the future. As a result, the brain might preserve vivid memories of negative events in which we felt shame so that we feel dread when approaching similar situations. Feelings like these help us from repeating disastrous choices.

No One Is an Island

The root of the word "shame" means to cover, or to hide. Because shame is so searing and uncomfortable, it's understandable that we'd want to hide, but doing so can lay the foundations for a private prison of toxic shame. The more you identify with shame, the more you'll isolate yourself. In these hiding places, we not only lose touch with who we really are, we lose touch with each other. These are dark places where we torture ourselves with cruel judgments and self-condemnations.

In establishing shame and dread as the guardians of the world, Buddhist psychology emphasizes that we are all in this together and are irrevocably intertwined. This point of view acknowledges that we must be mindful of feelings like healthy shame so as to not create suffering in our own lives or the lives of others. We are deeply connected in a web of relationships in which we influence and are influenced by others, though we may sometimes feel quite separate from even those closest to us. Mindfulness meditation and inquiry can help us gradually discover, or perhaps recover, a deep connectedness with others.

Dealing with Toxic Shame

Clearly, healthy shame serves a vital role, so it's important to learn how to distinguish between healthy shame and toxic shame. As you explore this question and specific feelings of shame, consider these questions: Are you judging a specific action, or are you judging yourself? Did you make certain mistakes, or do you think you're shameful in general? Are you learning from your mistakes, or do you think you're inherently terrible?

The deep roots of the word "suffer" mean to bear, or to carry, and of the many burdens we may carry, toxic shame is one of the heaviest. It's like a ton of bricks on your back, each formed from a self-condemnation, and together creating a harsh judgment of your entire being because of things you've done or haven't done. Yet these building blocks of toxic shame are so arbitrary. You may shame yourself because you haven't been able to overcome debt and give more to your family, or you may shame yourself for being wealthy while others suffer in poverty. You may feel shame about things you have absolutely no responsibility for, like your race or gender, or the failings of your parents or other family members—their addictions, their crimes, their apparent inability to love you or provide for you. You may even blame yourself for being abused, molested, or traumatized. It doesn't matter—it's possible to shame yourself for just about anything.

As you can see, the bricks of shame aren't necessarily horrible misdeeds, and in the end it isn't really about what you've done or haven't done; it's about how you blame yourself for those things in the stories you tell yourself about yourself.

Our individual stories of unworthiness are told in countless ways, but the story line remains the same: A painful event happened, the event was judged harshly, triggering powerful emotions, and this cycle repeated again and again, either in actual events or in memories and the imagination. As the emotion was triggered repeatedly, it transformed into a mood. The mood became pervasive, until eventually it created an attitude of mind that crystallized into a false self, fabricated from stories of unworthiness.

But is this sense of self really who you are? Remember, how you relate to your stories can make all the difference in whether they're poisonous or medicinal. You can become entangled with them and identify with them, or you can use them to inform skillful choices and actions as you move forward.

Digging your way out of toxic shame and the isolation it creates can feel like an overwhelming task, but it's truly just a matter of changing your perspective. In his book *Meditation in Action*, Chögyam Trungpa reported that Buddha said, "Unskilled farmers are those who throw away their rubbish and buy manure from other farmers, but those who are skilled go on collecting their own rubbish, in spite of the bad smell and the unclean work, and when it is ready to be used they spread it on their own land, and out of this they grow their crops" (Trungpa 1991, 21). In other words, the suggestion is that you gather the manure of your life and spread it on the field of your awakening. Bringing forth what is inside you may seem like an impossibly difficult act of self-disclosure, but it actually provides what's needed for new growth to flourish. That's why unflinchingly honest self-disclosure is such a key element in approaches like 12-step programs and the "confessional booth" of psychotherapy—and in mindful self-inquiry. Consider it to be a form of "light therapy," where your healing takes root in dark places and grows in the full light of awareness and self-compassion.

It takes courage to explore your mind. Each personal expedition inward is a hero's journey. Take heart and know that, no matter how painful or difficult, each new discovery is another step toward freedom. One mindful way of working with difficult emotions, including shame, is to let them be part of your meditation practice. There's no need to censor them or push them away. Simply acknowledge uncomfortable feelings as you practice. Although it can be scary, turning inward to the dark places allows you to open and heal your heart. Over time, as you dip your toes into and out of the cold water of your fears, you'll begin to acclimate to the temperature. Take it slowly, and hold yourself with gentleness and self-compassion throughout. In time you may recognize that there are teachers everywhere, as Rumi expressed so beautifully in his poem "The Guest House" (1997, 77):

This being human is a guest-house.
Every morning a new arrival.
A joy, a depression, a meanness,
some momentary awareness comes
as an unexpected visitor.
Welcome and entertain them all!
Even if they're a crowd of sorrows,
Who violently sweep your house
empty of its furniture.
Still, treat each guest honorably.
He may be clearing you out
for some new delight.
The dark thought, the shame, the malice,
meet them at the door laughing, and invite them in.
Be grateful for whoever comes,
because each has been sent
as a guide from beyond.

Mindfulness Practice: Formal Mindfulness Meditation

The mindfulness practices you've learned up to this point are all helpful in disidentifying with the narrative-based self. The body scan and mindfulness of the breath both help you fully inhabit your body in the here and now. Noting helps you create some space between yourself and your thoughts and emotions, and mindful self-inquiry helps illuminate the dark, long-unexamined places within you. Now we'll introduce mindfulness meditation, a practice that can give you a radical new perspective, helping you see that all body and mind states are impermanent and constantly changing. As you'll discover, it's much harder to identify with something once you understand that it's impermanent.

In mindfulness meditation, you bring awareness to your breath, then to physical sensations, then to sounds, then to thoughts or emotions, and finally to choiceless, or present moment, awareness. This is the most fluid of mindfulness meditation practices. You simply become mindful of whatever is arising in the present moment—whatever is prominent and distinct, whether sounds, sensations in the body, or thoughts, emotions, and other mind states. You witness them as ever-changing and impermanent phenomena, coming and going.

We've adapted the instructions for this exercise from *A Mindfulness-Based Stress Reduction Workbook*, by Bob Stahl and Elisha Goldstein (New Harbinger Publications, 2010). Read through the entire exercise before you begin. Give yourself thirty minutes for this practice. However, if you're short on time you can do less. As with the body scan, you may find it helpful to record the instructions and listen to the recording as you practice. You can also purchase a CD of this practice at www.yourheartwideopen.com. Soon enough you'll be familiar with the practice and won't need to listen to the instructions. Sit in a posture that's comfortable yet allows you to remain alert, and bring your full, undivided attention to this practice.

Begin with a mindful check-in, feeling into your physical sensations, thoughts, and emotions. Whatever you find, just let it be. This may be the first time you've slowed down today, so just allow whatever you're feeling to be present. There's no need to figure anything out or solve anything. Just acknowledge whatever is within you and let it be. Stay with the mindful check-in for about five minutes.

Gradually, shift the focus of awareness to the breath, breathing normally and naturally. As you breathe in, be aware of breathing in, as you breathe out, be aware of breathing out.

Focus your awareness at your nose, chest, belly, or wherever you feel the breath most prominently and distinctly. If focusing on the nose, feel the sensation of the air as you breathe in and out. If focusing on the chest or abdomen, feel it expanding with each inhalation and contracting with each exhalation, simply being mindful of how the breath feels in the body and experiencing life one inhalation and one exhalation at a time. Breathing in and out and witnessing how the breath ebbs and flows... Stay with the breath for about five minutes.

Now gently withdraw your focus from the breath and shift it to physical sensations. Become mindful of the changing nature of the sensations that rise and fall in the body. If no sensations are prominent, feel into the touch points where your body is making contact with the chair, cushion, or floor. Feel how the sensations are constantly shifting and changing. There's no need to judge or analyze sensations. Just let them be as they change from one moment to the next, feeling sensations in the body. Stay with sensations for about five minutes.

Now gently release your awareness of sensations and bring attention to sounds. There's no need to identify, analyze, judge, or interpret sounds. Simply be aware of sound at its most basic—an auditory phenomenon that's just as ephemeral as the breath or physical sensations. You may hear nearby sounds or sounds farther away. As your concentration deepens you may hear the internal sounds of the body, such as the breath, pulse, or heartbeat, or a ringing in your ears. Whether sounds arise within or without, they are just sounds, rising and falling. Stay with sounds for about five minutes.

Now gently shift attention from awareness of sounds to mind states, to thoughts and emotions. Allow yourself to experience how mind states come and go, just like the breath, sensations, and sounds. There's no need to figure them out or analyze them; they're just mental phenomena coming and going. Experience them appearing and disappearing, just thoughts and emotions.

As you become mindful of mind states, you may notice that the mind has a mind of its own. It's constantly analyzing, comparing, contrasting, liking, disliking, remembering, or planning, or filled with a multitude of emotions. Just allow mind states to come and go, and observe their transience…just mind states rolling on and on… If you find that you've gotten lost in thoughts and emotions rather than being mindful of them, simply return to the breath to build concentration and awareness, then shift your focus back to mind states. Stay with mind states for about five minutes.

Now gently withdraw awareness from mental states and bring your attention to the present moment itself as the primary object of attention. Simply watch the changing phenomena that present themselves—sensory experiences, thoughts, and emotions. Just sit back and be mindful of the ever-shifting tides of mind and body. Even as you are sitting still, your body and mind are fluid and dynamic, constantly changing.

See yourself as sitting by the edge of a stream and just watching whatever's coming downstream. Sometimes there are sounds, sometimes sensations, sometimes thoughts and emotions. If nothing much is occurring, you can always come back to the anchor of the breath. If something painful is occurring, go with it rather than fighting it. Give difficult thoughts and emotions space to simply be. Stay with choiceless awareness for about five minutes.

Now gently withdraw from choiceless awareness and come back to the breath, feeling the entire body as it breathes in and out. Feel the body rising upward on an inhalation and descending on an exhalation. Feel the body as a single organism, connected and whole.

As you come to the end of this meditation, congratulate yourself for giving yourself this gift of time. May you know that you are directly contributing to your health and well-being.

Take a little time to write in your journal about what you encountered in this practice. What time of day did you do it? How long did you stay with it? How did you deal with hindrances like restlessness or drowsiness? What did you notice about your thoughts, emotions, and sensations? Writing a little in your journal after each meditation practice can be a skillful way to hone your practice and make it increasingly beneficial.

As you continue to practice mindfulness meditation, you'll come to see that life is a flow, and the more you resist that flow, the more pain you'll experience. This practice will also help you develop more equanimity and balance. So even if you're experiencing storms of unworthiness, inadequacy, anxiety, sadness, anger, or confusion, you can let them be and acknowledge them. Like all other phenomena, these emotions come and go, and when you give them the space they need, they may subside more quickly.

Understanding the ephemeral and changing nature of your mind and body can also be very powerful in liberating you from entanglement with limiting stories about yourself. It offers a vantage point from which you can notice new or unexpected things about yourself, others, and all the experiences of your life, and this frees you to respond in new ways.

Savoring This Journey

In this chapter you learned two new mindfulness practices: mindful self-inquiry and formal mindfulness meditation. In mindful self-inquiry, you turn the focus of the awareness you've cultivated in previous practices to difficult thoughts and emotions, and specifically those involved in pervasive feelings of unworthiness. Though this work is challenging, know that it offers profound healing as you begin to use spacious awareness to help you disidentify from painful thoughts and emotions and self-limiting stories about yourself. Mindful self-inquiry also gives you a chance to practice disentangling yourself from the traps of the narrative-based self by focusing on the immediacy of the present moment. For the next few weeks, practice mindful self-inquiry frequently. With time and practice, it can help you develop new ways of responding to painful feelings, rather than reacting in habitual ways.

Formal mindfulness meditation is a way of returning to beginner's mind again and again. It also offers an extraordinarily profound and healing insight: that all phenomena and experiences are ephemeral. Understanding that everything is impermanent—that "this too shall pass"—helps soften difficult experiences and build acceptance. At the same time, it heightens the awareness of just how precious each fleeting moment is. The awareness you cultivate in this practice is truly the essence of mindfulness. We recommend that you make formal mindfulness meditation an ongoing practice for the rest of your life.

Chapter 5

~

Opening to Self-Compassion

Be gentle with yourself. Be kind to yourself. You may not be perfect, but you are all you've got to work with. The process of becoming who you will be begins first with the total acceptance of who you are.

—Bhante Henepola Gunaratana

As you've learned, a pervasive sense of unworthiness is typically maintained with stories you tell yourself that describe you as a personality. These stories and the narrative-based self they create may sometimes enable you to escape the pain of unwanted and disowned feelings, but they build a faulty identity that feels alienated and separate from others, and they create what meditation teacher and psychologist Tara Brach calls "the trance of unworthiness" (2004, 5).

Buddhist psychology regards the notion of a separate and fixed self, a self that endures over time, as a misconception. When we maintain this misconception with the stories we repeatedly tell ourselves, we create a type of suffering that eclipses the original pain. Some tenets of Western psychology parallel this fundamental assertion of Buddhist psychology. For example, psychologist Albert Ellis, considered by many to be the father of cognitive behavioral psychology, asserted that the statements we tell ourselves create the greatest part of our suffering, particularly the things we say to ourselves when we believe we've done something wrong (Ellis 1969). He identified self-blame as the core of what we refer to as toxic shame in this book ("Because I did this mistaken act, I'm no good as a human being"). Ellis emphasized the fundamental difference between a regrettable act and a damaged identity. Doing something bad and being someone bad are different things. Telling ourselves we're no good because we've done something wrong is a surefire way to induce the numbing trance of unworthiness.

Because the stories we tell ourselves often serve to insulate us from our feelings, healing begins as soon as we welcome these rejected feelings back into our lives. A beginning meditation practice is often the place where this work starts, as these painful and unwanted feelings often make themselves known by rudely intruding into what we expected to be a peaceful sojourn of meditative bliss. In those moments, it also becomes immediately evident how quickly our stories of an inadequate self arise the moment we get near these painful feelings, as if to help us escape from emotions we are not yet ready to embrace.

Pain is intrinsic to our lives. It's inescapable, yet escape is one of our first impulses when we encounter painful things that we cannot change. When all else fails, we may try to escape by detaching ourselves from remembering, an act of mind called *dissociation*. In this state of mind we don't have to feel what is happening or has happened to us. For this very reason, all addictions serve to deepen this emotionally numbing trance.

Most of us are familiar with efforts to avoid feeling emotional pain. Many of us have been taught not to cry, even when extremely sad things happen, like the loss of a family member. It seems we often do everything we can to avoid feeling our pain, and while this may work in the moment, the wounded and forsaken heart can never heal in its lonely exile. It never stops longing for love and compassion.

The heart you have abandoned is still waiting where you left it, and within it is all the vitality you lost when you turned away from your pain. Self-compassion allows you to open the door to your heart and welcome the vitality and guidance of your feelings back into your awareness. With self-compassion, you can learn to comfort and heal the pain you once banished.

What Is Self-Compassion?

To understand self-compassion, it may be helpful to take a look at compassion in the larger sense, as we experience it with others. First, let's take a look at the word itself. The prefix "com" means "with," and the deep roots of the word "passion" mean "to suffer." So the word "compassion" expresses an act of joining with suffering. To practice compassion is to turn toward suffering with an open and caring heart that looks for a way to alleviate suffering. As you turn toward the suffering of others, you realize that no one wants to suffer, that everyone wants to be happy and at peace, just like you do. If nothing else can be done to soothe a troubled heart, sometimes just caring enough to stay and be with it is a powerful healing balm.

It may be easier to understand the healing power of compassion when you reflect on the moments in your life when others responded to you with compassion, even in the smallest of ways. Perhaps you were being snubbed at school and a girl you didn't even know befriended you, or maybe someone in the doctor's waiting room saw how terrible you felt and suggested that you see the doctor first.

Self-compassion is giving to yourself what you would like others to give to you. It means being kind and caring with yourself, rather than harsh or critical. It means being with painful thoughts and feelings without overidentifying with them or making them into a story about you. It's a way to accept yourself even though you are not perfect. As you learn to be with unpleasant emotions, they may call forth difficult memories, perhaps created in your earliest life relationships. Each memory, no matter how painful, delivers another piece of your heart to itself. Welcome them all—the memories, the emotions, and all the formerly rejected parts of yourself. This not only allows you to reclaim your wholeness, it also reveals a deep connectedness with others. For as you learn to be with your own suffering, you'll gradually come see that your pain is like everyone else's. The more deeply you can connect with your own heart, the more deeply you'll be able to connect with every other heart. Of course this doesn't happen overnight. This is a path of gradual awakening, and patience and nonstriving will support you a great deal in this work.

For many of us, self-compassion is harder to find than compassion for others. Most people say they're less kind and more critical toward themselves than they are toward others (Neff and McGehee 2008). Yet in Buddhist psychology, self-compassion is considered equally important as compassion for others. In fact, compassion and loving-kindness practices traditionally begin with self-compassion. This may seem strange or even self-indulgent at first, but it's healing to give ourselves what our hearts have always longed for, and this healing can soften the barriers between ourselves and others. After all, our physical hearts infuse themselves with blood before sending blood to other parts of the body. If you fill yourself with self-compassion, you may be able to extend more compassion to others.

Interestingly, research on self-compassion has demonstrated that, compared to people with less self-compassion, those with more self-compassion are more likely to forgive others. They're also more likely to take other people's perspectives yet feel less distress when doing so (Neff and McGehee 2008). We believe that the converse is also true: that compassion you feel toward others can also help you feel more compassion for yourself. No matter which way it flows, compassion is like a stream that grows larger as its channel deepens.

The Trap of Self-Improvement

In the healing work of self-compassion, it's important to avoid the trap of getting caught up in self-improvement. When you have a pervasive sense of unworthiness, this can be tricky. The identity of unworthiness is formed of self-blame and a deluge of self-judgments offered by an inner critic who wants nothing to do with self-compassion. It's far more interested in masochistic endeavors like self-improvement projects that it's never satisfied with. But this just gets you more stuck in feeling deficient for several reasons, the foremost being the very idea that there's a faulty and unworthy self that needs to be improved.

As discussed, Buddhist psychology asserts that the very concept of a static and enduring self is the most profound of delusions and the source of endless suffering. Believing that you can fix the unworthy self just leaves you trapped in the never-ending pursuit of being "good enough" through better workshops, new therapies, or a better diet or exercise program. In many ways it's no different from always striving for more money or more things. It's just another variation on eternally wanting something more or better.

Here's how the trap works: Setting a goal of a better self calls forth wanting. Wanting calls forth striving. Striving calls forth judging. And judging becomes a way of life that brings a critical orientation to everything: "Oh, I like that! Oh, I don't like that! Oh, that's good! Oh, that's bad!" It never stops, and while the mind is thus engaged, it isn't in the here and now; it's preoccupied with getting somewhere else. This craving to be somehow better can fill up a lifetime yet never be fulfilled.

Remember, this moment truly is the time of your life, and what's important is to be here for it, to actually live in the here and now. There is no other moment to live in. The mind that's perennially striving for a better place or condition creates suffering by leaving the present moment, which is the only place we can experience love, peace, or happiness. When you are somewhere other than now, you can miss the most precious experiences of your life. This can be akin to searching for your camera to preserve an experience that you end up missing because you're searching for the camera. A mind that is extended toward the future is focused on some goal, and even if this goal is reached, the striving mind will then measure how the new condition compares with the past, thus ensuring that you remain perennially preoccupied with the past and future and rarely, if ever, actually live in the here and now.

Living in the present moment doesn't mean that you discard your goals, whether that means having a nice car that's paid for, moving your family to a better home or safer neighborhood, or losing weight. It means remaining oriented to the here and now as you work toward what you want.

The judging mind can always find something that isn't quite right, particularly when it's looking from this nebulous thing called "self." We tend to get the standards by which we judge ourselves by looking around and comparing ourselves to others. But if you consider how many billions of people there are on this planet, you can see that this is a no-win proposition. There will always be someone thinner, fitter, nicer, more accomplished, more attractive, more popular—whatever.

Noticing what you do with your mind and these comparisons can help you see how much suffering is caused by this endless stream of judgments and the violence of self-criticism. You may hate your potbelly and want to get rid of it, or you may despise the way you chicken out and fail to say what you really think. But hating and criticizing things about yourself only creates more suffering. This is like a military strategy based on the idea that war can create peace—that if you can blast the inadequate self to smithereens, or maybe just threaten to do so, you will finally feel okay and have peace. This way of thinking just etches the neurological pathways of suffering more deeply into your brain and colors your thoughts with narratives about what's wrong with you and how you need to improve.

The way to peace is never through war, and the way to happiness is never through hatred. Peace is the way to peace, and happiness comes from happiness. If you want compassion to grow in your life, practice compassion. If you want criticism to grow in your life, practice criticism. It's simple, really: Your attitude is the water of your life. You can promote feelings of inadequacy and unworthiness by pouring on self-blame and criticism, or you can promote feelings of happiness and well-being by pouring on self-compassion.

The quality of your attitude is influenced by many things, but especially by your mood and your orientation to life itself. If you have a critical orientation, you'll find unlimited things to criticize and may find yourself caught in the trap of self-improvement for much of your life. If you have a compassionate orientation, you'll find many opportunities for compassion and may discover freedom and happiness in your life right now. The attitude of self-compassion can grow even as you're attending to your pain and woundedness, or even as you reflect on mistakes you've made that hurt you or others. You grow self-compassion by practicing self-compassion, just like a pianist becomes more skilled by practicing the piano. Small errors, such as forgetting something at the store, or large errors, like forgetting your wedding anniversary, can become opportunities for you to grow a little more in self-kindness and self-compassion.

Yes, there are many tears to cry, as well as embarrassing errors and sometimes shameful choices to take responsibility for, but even as you're shaken to the core by difficult emotions that flood through you, you can attend to your wounded heart with acceptance and self-compassion. In this way you can enhance the values you would like to grow in yourself, even as you attend to suffering with friendly and kind attention. In time, suffering subsides, just like a child's tears subside after she's been rocked and sung to enough. As the pain is lifted, her face changes and becomes beautiful with the calm after the storm. Know that for you too there will come a time when you have cried yourself to the end of your tears and a feeling of peace surrounds and embraces you. This is one of the greatest treasures of mindfulness and self-compassion.

The Hidden and Wounded Child

Looking deeply into the repetitive and dysfunctional habits of our lives, we often find that they're driven by a greater pain—one that all of the chaos we've created serves to obscure. The source of this pain is often an innocent and wounded heart that has long been hidden and disowned. It's an act of self-compassion to simply look for and be with this wounded innocence with kind awareness and presence. Consider the way a loving mother holds her crying infant and studies his face to try to understand why he is so unhappy. Everything in her heart longs to comfort her baby, to understand his pain and help him in some way. She aches for him. Be this way with yourself.

This allows you to turn toward the suffering in your own heart without falling apart. Don't look away; don't fall into the same old swarm of self-protecting feelings again. Your capacity for self-compassion is greater than you may realize, and you can hold this ache in your heart. Turn toward your suffering with awareness and loving-kindness. Look for ways to regard yourself with tenderness and compassion. Each time you return to this place, your self-compassion may grow a little more, allowing you to emerge from the numbing trance of unworthiness a bit more.

It All Comes Down to Love

We've discussed some of the ways in which we deepen and perpetuate habits of mind by repeating them. Up to this point, we've discussed this process in regard to its downside: creating the narrative-based self and limiting self-concepts. Yet this process also has an upside—something Henry David Thoreau spoke to over 150 years ago: "As a single footstep will not make a path on the earth, so a single thought will not make a pathway in the mind. To make a deep physical path, we walk again and again. To make a deep mental path, we must think over and over the kind of thoughts we wish to dominate our lives" (2006, 27).

Thoreau's experiential wisdom has been confirmed by recent neurological research conducted by Richard Davidson at the University of Wisconsin (Davidson et al. 2003; Davidson 2009). With every experience, particularly emotional experiences, your brain rewires, changing its physical structure and creating new neurological pathways that grow stronger (like paths that grow deeper) as we think them and feel them over and over again.

Dr. Davidson's research demonstrated that we can intentionally shape our brains and change our emotional traits in beneficial ways and that these skills are trainable. The brain scan studies in his research showed that people who had participated in an eight-week mindfulness-based stress reduction program had increased activity in their left prefrontal lobe—an area of the brain linked to positive emotions, good mood, and self-control. In addition, they experienced less anxiety and showed significant improvement in immune functioning. This goes to show that as little as eight weeks of training in mindfulness meditation and loving-kindness practice can improve your ability to enjoy life. In his closing remarks at a conference in 2009, Dr. Davidson said, "It all comes down to love," an interesting summation from one of the foremost neuroscientists in the world (Davidson 2009).

Never underestimate the powers of love, and consider that even one lit candle in the night illuminates and dispels the darkness. There's an ancient Buddhist proverb that states, "Hatred never ceases by hatred; it only ceases by love. This is a timeless truth" (Goldstein 2003, 125).

We're All in This Together

Because we are all interconnected, if even one human mind can be transformed by love in this way, perhaps that will create a ripple by which many more lives are transformed. We human beings influence each other in ways large and small for better and for worse. If one heart closes, many others may also close. If one heart awakens, many others may also awaken.

Have you ever been stuck at an airport or anywhere else for a long time with a bunch of other people? Because you have no choice but to surrender to the current circumstances, you're temporarily freed from the typical goal-oriented drive of trying to get somewhere on time. In these circumstances, you can begin to see the people around you differently. You might strike up conversations or find things in common, and then find yourself looking at the situation differently. Where you had been stuck and annoyed, you might look around and see that you're all in this together—you aren't alone in your frustration with the situation.

In moments like these, you may realize that everyone has to cope with problems, and often the same kind of problems you face. We all have to find a way to cope with the pain of disappointment, frustration, failure, and loss, and none of us is exempt from suffering. This universal aspect of compassion can do much to free you from the trance of unworthiness.

Just as developing self-compassion contributes to your ability to feel compassion for others, seeing that we're all in this together, all at the mercy of circumstances or the human condition, contributes to your ability to feel compassion for yourself. Rather than isolating yourself with a story that you're somehow fundamentally different and fatally flawed, you see that others have similar experiences. With time, you can learn to extend to yourself the same type of acceptance and kindness that you might extend to others.

Cultivating Self-Compassion

Self-compassion entails softening around the heart and giving yourself a break from self-judgment with kindness and caring. Understand that criticizing yourself (or others) is a source of suffering and is an entirely optional activity of the thinking mind.

It may not seem like it at this time, but as you travel the path of mindfulness and self-compassion, you'll eventually discover that there is much more right with you than there is wrong. Sometimes we can find what's right and wholesome and worthwhile within us only after we've opened to and allowed ourselves to feel the pain we've been avoiding. The site of a wound is eventually the place of healing, and the way a heart mends is no less wondrous than the way a skinned knee mends. If you attend your wounded heart with compassion, the healing will tend to itself. If you attend your wounded heart with negative judgment, it will stoke the flames of suffering.

You can practice tender loving care with yourself in all the circumstances of your life. You may wonder how to begin. Try this: The next time you do something that you perceive as wrong or embarrassing, turn to yourself as a kind parent turns to a child, with words like "Bless your heart. I know how bad this must feel. I'm sorry that you're going through this." Then, consider feeling more deeply into the emotion that's filling you, and even consider putting your hand on the place in your body that feels this emotion the most. Say to yourself, "Of course it feels awful! Nobody likes to mess up or face the consequences of unskillful actions." In this way, you can hold yourself with kindness and let yourself know that you are loved even when you're hurting and unhappy. Remind yourself that everyone makes mistakes, and stay tenderly present with yourself until you feel the pain subside. Compassion may help you face whatever happened with more awareness, so you gain more insight into how you might act more skillfully in the future.

These expressions of kindness are all the more healing when you can bring them to the hurt and frightened child within yourself and extend self-compassion for injuries or wounds that happened long ago. As you look deeply into your patterns of self-blame and shame, you might become excruciatingly aware of how those you relied on as a child let you down. Stay with these feelings, turning toward the anguish of the abandoned child rather than trying to push away your feelings.

If you can learn to respond to this suffering with acceptance and kindness rather than avoidance, a river of grief and pain can begin to pour out of the places in your heart that have lain hidden behind self-blame for so many years. By staying compassionately with this anguish, you'll find that the self-judgments you've been living with for so long have been a substitute for the difficult feelings that are coming up, serving to obscure them. Holding yourself with the arms of com-passion, you can tell yourself, "No wonder you've been so angry and unhappy. It was just too painful for a child to accept. But it wasn't your fault that these things happened to you, and you were so brave to do as well as you did." Self-compassion is giving yourself what others may not have been able to give you, as Rumi so well says in this brief poem (2010, 351):

A pearl goes up for auction. No one has enough,
so the pearl buys itself.

Self-compassion enables you to be just who you are, where you are, and as you are by giving you a means to be with your pain rather than spinning out stories about it. Compassion arises from mindful presence and awareness as you attend to pain as an inevitable part of life. The open heart extends self-compassion to every part of your being, even the internal critic that judges you so mercilessly.

As you disidentify from your internal critic and your sense of inad-equacy or sense of being a victim and refocus from the perspective of nonjudging mindful awareness, you can see that it's possible to choose a compassionate response rather than a critical reaction to what you witness in the world within and around you. Often, criticism and anger arise from what Daniel Siegel refers to in his book *The Mindful Brain* (2007) as a "top-down" orientation, originating in a mentally domi-nated or narrative-based sense of self. Compassion arises from what he calls a "bottom-up" orientation, originating in the body and the heart. These orientations are simply habits, and which you operate from is entirely optional.

The Many Paths to Self-Compassion

Investigating how you can cultivate self-compassion in your life involves an exploration of how you relate to your body, thoughts, and emotions, and also how you choose and maintain your relationships. Considering how we can be more compassionate toward our bodies can help many of us see how very little compassion we have for ourselves and how hard we push ourselves physically. You may find yourself answering yet another e-mail even though you've needed to use the bathroom for over an hour, or you may eat junk food from the nearest source just so you can get back to work sooner. You may convince yourself that you don't have time to exercise, or you may have a somewhat perverse sense of pride in how little sleep you get. Paying attention to the many ways you mistreat your body can provide a great deal of insight into how you can begin practicing self-compassion right now—simply by reversing many of these habits.

It's the same with thoughts and emotions. You can learn to witness unpleasant thoughts and emotions with self-compassion, and even come to feel a certain amount of compassion for the inner critic (which often helps calm this eternal source of self-criticism). When you notice that you're being hard on yourself for something like being late for an appointment, you can turn toward this self-criticism with a soft and kind acknowledgement, like "It's only a mistake; I love you anyway." If you notice that you're ruminating on a feeling like guilt and saying things to yourself that are just making you feel more guilty, you can acknowledge this morbid indulgence; for example, you might say, "This is just a guilt-fest" or "Will heaping on even more guilt really help me learn from this mistake?" For most of us, learning to attend to our thoughts and emotions with this friendly kind of attention is a very different way of being in the world.

Caring for ourselves in relationships with others is another way to cultivate self-compassion. Do you really need to remain in relationships that make you feel small or less alive? Do you really need to accommodate yet another phone conversation with the "friend" who calls you only when she needs advice or reassurance? Do you always have to accommodate lunch invitations from a coworker who likes to gossip about the other people in your workplace? Why not try discouraging relationships that feel like they deplete you and nourishing relationships that make you feel loved and appreciated and bring out the best in you? We are meant to love one another and care for one another in the deepest sense, and cultivating relationships that manifest these qualities is the very heart of self-compassion.

Exercise: Cultivating Self-Compassion

As mentioned, for most people self-compassion is more difficult than extending compassion to others. So in this exercise, you'll cultivate self-compassion by considering what sort of support you'd offer to a friend in your situation.

> If you met with a friend and she confided in you that she felt completely worthless and ashamed, how would you try to comfort her? What would you tell her to soothe her troubled heart? In what other ways would you express your loving-kindness and compassion? Take a few moments to reflect on this, and then spend some time writing in your journal about what you'd say to your friend.
>
> Now consider some ways you too have felt sad or unhappy, and offer yourself words of compassion that are similar to what you would offer your friend.
>
> Notice what happens in your body and mind as you offer these expressions of compassion and loving-kindness to yourself. Pay attention to what comes up for you physically, mentally, and emotionally. Turn toward your own aching heart and perhaps even place your hand on your chest, and then acknowledge to yourself, "I care for this suffering." Feel deeply into this suffering and inquire into the attitude you would have toward a friend or loved one who was going though this.
>
> Know that all human beings have to cope with suffering in their lives, and that many others have suffered in the way you are now suffering. As you feel into this truth of being human,

you can find a sense of connection with others that dispels the isolating trance that personal suffering can induce. Understand that no one is exempt from suffering.

Breathe into the tight places in your body, inviting a little more tension to release with each exhalation. Be tender and caring even toward whatever comments arise from your internal critic. Simply allow unkind thoughts to come and go and know that these probably arise from fear, and that, like all other phenomena, they too will pass. Turn toward any hurt feelings with self-compassion, and use this time to be with yourself with loving-kindness. From time to time, repeat to yourself, "I care for this suffering."

Bring this exercise to a close by practicing mindful breathing for about ten minutes. Offer yourself gratitude and congratulations for giving yourself this gift of mindfulness and self-compassion.

Take a little time to write in your journal about your experience with this exercise. How did it feel to treat yourself with compassion?

Sometimes we must grow in compassion for others before we can discover compassion for ourselves. When you think of others with a sense of compassion, your heart widens. This is also true when you think of yourself with a sense of caring. Your heart widens like a ripe pomegranate widens—so filled with caring and compassion it actually bursts out of its shell.

Mindfulness Practice: Self-Compassion Meditation

This practice builds on the mindful self-inquiry practice you learned in chapter 4, which helps you to turn toward even painful feelings with an open heart, and to welcome them rather than flee from them. Self-compassion allows you to be with and care for your own woundedness and pain and live with your heart wide open. The moment you embrace the disowned and wounded parts of yourself, the husks of your old narrative-based self can fall away.

All of us sometimes act unskillfully and make poor choices that hurt others, and we are all sometimes hurt by the actions of others. Rather than pushing thoughts and feelings about these things away, and rather than trying to correct anything or anyone, simply be with the thoughts and feelings that come up for you with curiosity and awareness. As you practice self-compassion meditation, the intention is to be open to all of your thoughts, emotions, and sensations, to let all the streams of perception flow through you unfettered. It's a practice of being with yourself just as you are.

Review the AWARE practice in chapter 4 before doing the following meditation. Give yourself at least thirty minutes for this practice. Choose a place to practice where you feel safe and at ease. If you like, place some objects that are special and comforting to you on a shelf nearby, or light a candle or arrange some flowers in this space that you create for yourself. Know that you're giving yourself a gift of love.

Begin by practicing mindfulness of breathing for ten minutes, returning to the breath with self-compassion every time you leave it. Throughout this entire practice, use the AWARE practice from chapter 4 (allow, witness, acknowledge, release, and ease up) to work with thoughts and emotions that come up for you. Let your thoughts and emotions come and go. Being present...

Staying in touch with your breath, recall one of the strongest emotions that came up for you during the ten minutes of mindful breathing. If no strong emotions came up for you, simply recall a recent experience of strong emotions. Notice what happens in your body as you feel this emotion and breathe into any parts of your body that are affected. Be open to and present with any other emotions that may come up. Perhaps shame feels like a rope wrapped around your chest that keeps getting tighter and makes it hard to breathe. What does the emotion you're having feel like? By feeling more deeply into it, you may discover other thoughts and emotions—perhaps self-hatred that reaches into your gut, where it churns and twists and hurts. Keep paying attention. Feel more deeply into what's happening and stay present in your body. Let whatever happens in your mind and body happen. Notice if old unwanted memories that have lain hidden arise. If they do, let them come, and notice how they feel in the body.

Let everything be in this unrestricted kind of attention; don't block anything out. Don't let the trance of unworthiness swallow your heart. Stay near the pain with compassion. It's the awakened heart that stays with and heals. It's all happening right here and now, where your body is. Stay with everything you're experiencing, and remember that this practice is about offering compassion to yourself and feeling that compassion. It's not about figuring anything out or fixing or getting rid of anything. Remember, it all comes down to love, including love for yourself. It all comes down to what you're doing in this moment. Use the breath as your way to remain anchored in the present moment, letting it come and go as it will.

In the same way that you allow your breath to come and go freely, allow your emotions to come and go freely. Notice any judgments that come up for you as you allow strong or unwanted emotions to arise. Notice how the judgments affect your emotions, perhaps blocking them or washing them out, perhaps calling forth other emotions. Welcome all of your emotions as you observe and acknowledge the judgments without indulging them.

Be with whatever emotions come up for you with compassion. Welcome each with kindness and meet all of them with gentleness and tenderness. Hold yourself in the arms of self-compassion and be present with what you feel. Stay with this practice and your emotions for as long as you like.

When you're ready to end this practice, return to practicing mindfulness of the breath for ten minutes.

Offer a measure of gratitude to yourself for taking the time to care for yourself in this way.

Take a little time to write in your journal about what came up for you in this practice. Write about any emotions you noticed being attached to one another, such as helplessness bringing up fear, or fear evoking anger. Write about all of the emotions that came up for you here and whether or how they changed when you held them with self-compassion.

As you continue to practice self-compassion, you may notice more and more things about the self you've created with all of your old stories. Perhaps you tried to be especially good to counterbalance the problems in your family. Perhaps you learned to be generous of yourself as a way of earning the value you felt you lacked. Self-compassion lets you be with all of the hurt, loneliness, and fear that the narrative-based self has concealed. In the wide-open heart of self-compassion, the wounded child within you will begin to heal.

Savoring This Journey

In this chapter we presented a self-compassion meditation, which will help you care for your wounded heart. Opening to yourself with kindness and tenderness will help you transform old wounds into sites of profound healing. Embracing this practice will bring you a sense of wholeness and self-acceptance you might have thought impossible. We recommend that you practice this meditation frequently over the next few weeks, for it is much like Thoreau's concept of a deep mental pathway that grows through repetition. And because the pathway of compassion is expansive, not unidirectional, as you develop more self-compassion, you'll also grow in your capacity to extend loving-kindness and compassion to others. As time goes on, continue to practice self-compassion meditation any time you notice that you're falling back into old, habitual, self-limiting stories of unworthiness or shame. Remember, self-compassion is one of the eight foundations of mindfulness. It's also essential to living with your heart wide open.

Chapter 6

~

Opening to Loving-Kindness

How did the rose ever open its heart
and give to this world all its beauty?
It felt the encouragement of light against its being,
otherwise, we all remain too frightened.

—Hafiz

In the previous chapter you learned several practices for cultivating self-compassion. The word "practice" is so fitting. These are things that you need to work with, just as you'd practice a musical instrument. As discussed in chapter 5, research in neuroscience has revealed that the repetition of practices like mindfulness and loving-kindness can help us establish new traits (Davidson 2009). Perhaps that's why meditation teacher Mary Grace Orr, a colleague of ours, often suggests a one-hundred-day loving-kindness practice for her students. She says that by the time you get to the hundredth day of practicing loving-kindness for yourself and others, you might actually experience it.

We want to affirm that you can develop new ways of seeing yourself and the world that will help you live with an open heart. From our perspective, living with an open heart means having your heart broken open to love. It means being fully open to everything in the present moment and learning to embrace it all—the good, the bad, the ugly, and all of the thoughts and emotions in the endless parade of the ten thousand joys and sorrows. This is difficult work. It's a bold move to open your heart to your fears and other painful thoughts and emotions, but there may come a time when you realize there's nothing more important to do, because living with a hardened or hidden heart is too great a pain to bear.

Embracing all of these experiences involves a certain type of trust that you've been building through your direct experience of mindfulness. You began this work of opening your heart with the self-compassion practices in the previous chapter. In this chapter we'll help you further open your heart with practices of loving-kindness, reconciliation, and empathetic joy.

∼ Howard's Story

Howard was plagued by anxiety that began the moment he woke up in the morning and stayed with him until he fell asleep at night. Sometimes it also kept him up at night. He felt as if he'd been wracked with these feelings forever, and he remembered being nervous and unsure of himself even as a boy. Whenever he encountered an uncomfortable social situation, he usually broke into a sweat, felt his heart rate go up, and started to breathe rapidly. He tended to flee these sorts of situations, and with time he began to avoid them altogether.

Howard despised how he dealt with his life and felt cowardly and inadequate. He felt so lonely, and so uncomfortable inside his own skin. And as if it weren't bad enough to feel so flawed and hopeless, he was starting to feel increasingly sleep deprived and stressed-out. He didn't want to take sleep aids or antianxiety medications, so when he read that mindfulness-based stress reduction might help, he was intrigued and signed up for a class.

In his first class, Howard realized that he wasn't alone in his struggle, and just knowing that many other people were also plagued by anxiety gave him some immediate relief. He was impressed that people had the guts to introduce themselves to the class and say out loud that they lived with anxiety. When his turn came, he also mustered up the courage to share about his situation, and afterward he felt an incredible lightness within himself. He also felt proud of himself for having the fortitude to speak up and tell his truth, and this gave him the first glimmer of hope he'd had in a long time.

As the weeks passed and Howard witnessed others opening to their fears and feeling freer from them, it gave him the courage to begin to face his own fears. As his mindfulness practice grew, he began to look more deeply into his fears and pain. He finally began to acknowledge his painful childhood and understand how and why he had lost so much confidence and felt so scared about life. When he was just eight years old, his younger brother had died, and that caused him to fear for his own safety and the safety of other loved ones. As these feelings became ingrained, his world was dominated by fear and mistrust. This had made him different and hard to get to know and helped explain why he'd had trouble making friends and why so many kids had picked on him back then.

Getting back in touch with the grief and pain that had been locked in his heart also helped him understand why he'd felt incompetent at school. School hadn't made much sense because he was dealing with bigger issues. While he was grappling with the meaning of life, and its impermanence, he couldn't relate to learning about anything else.

Howard's heart began to break open as he acknowledged his emotional pain and fear. As he understood the suffering of his younger self, he felt great compassion for that boy—self-compassion for his younger self. And, in part because of the stories others in his class had shared, he also realized that many people experience similar losses and similar struggles. These insights awakened his heart to great compassion and love.

What Is Loving-Kindness Meditation?

Loving-kindness is a meditation practice that involves sending unconditional love and goodwill to oneself and all beings. This practice is the embodiment of friendliness and nondiscrimination and opens the heart to the sublime qualities of altruistic love. It's a powerful antidote for the unworthy heart. Opening your heart to compassion and loving-kindness for yourself and then others will help you dissolve feelings of inadequacy, inferiority, and disconnection. We have known many people who found deep healing through this heartfelt practice.

The light of loving-kindness can be compared to that of the stars, the sun, or the moon. It shines on all living beings everywhere, encompassing them all without exception or bias. When practicing the loving-kindness meditation, you can direct this generous, unconditioned love to all beings inhabiting this earth. Eventually, you can extend it throughout the universe to all beings, even those yet to be born. This is a beautiful practice that opens the heart and cherishes all beings everywhere.

Exercise: Feeling Safe

The practice of loving-kindness begins with extending well-wishes to yourself and then gradually expands outward to others. Because it's a process of opening your heart, it's important that you feel safe as you practice. After all, if you don't feel safe, you may become confrontational or defensive, and this makes it difficult to open your heart with loving-kindness. You may have good reasons to feel unsafe. Perhaps you've been hurt badly in the past and now find it hard to trust others.

It's normal to want to protect yourself, so we'd like to offer you a practice to work with this.

> Take a moment right now to feel into your body and mind. Notice how you feel physically, mentally, and emotionally. Are you feeling safe or not? Take a few minutes to write in your journal about how you're feeling. What physical sensations do you feel? What thoughts or emotions are associated with these sensations?
>
> If you are feeling unsafe, are you open to exploring that feeling right now? If you aren't open to exploring this right now, please take care of yourself and do whatever you need to do to feel safe.
>
> If you are up for a closer look at why you aren't feeling safe, begin by acknowledging how you're feeling. Allow yourself to feel any physical, mental, or emotional experiences that come up for you, and just let them be. Let the waves of these experiences ripple or resonate wherever they need to go, simply giving space to whatever is.
>
> As you let these experiences be, you'll come to see that whatever arises passes away. You'll also come to understand what's fueling the feeling that you aren't safe. In time this insight can help set you free.
>
> Feel into your skin, flesh, and bones—your body sitting here and now in this room. Know that you are in a safe place, and that there is no danger in opening your heart... Breathing in and out, and opening to feeling safe.
>
> Are you feeling safe now? Can you ease into yourself right now and feel safe?

Take some time to write in your journal about what came up for you physically, mentally, and emotionally when you were doing this exercise. Were you able to enter into a place of feeling safe? If not, what did you do to take care of yourself? How are you feeling right now, after writing about your experience?

Cultivating a sense of safety helps nurture the conditions for practicing loving-kindness meditation. When you feel safe inside your being, it's easier to open your heart to extend love to yourself and to others.

∼ Jose's Story

Jose had a lot of anger. It seemed like he was pissed off at just about everything he encountered, and he felt that life was treating him unfairly. He didn't like his coworkers, didn't like how people drove, didn't like to fold the laundry or wash the dishes, didn't like waiting at red lights, and especially didn't like his girlfriend asking him to be kinder.

When his boss recommended anger management classes, Jose thought he didn't need them. And when a respected friend recommended a mindfulness-based stress reduction program, Jose said he thought mindfulness was a bunch of crap. But his life wasn't working. He'd gotten a couple of warnings for blowing up at coworkers and his job was on the line. Then his girlfriend said she wasn't sure she could stay in the relationship if things didn't change. Remembering his friend's advice, Jose decided to sign up for an MBSR program.

When he began practicing the body scan, he couldn't even feel his body because he was so disconnected from it. But with continued practice, he began reconnecting with his body. He found a lot of muscular tightness in the process, and in time, that tension led him to his anger. In his day-to-day life, he began to see that the aching neck and shoulders he'd discovered in the body scan usually started to show up when he felt frustrated and impatient, and the tense, locked jaw usually showed up right before he blew his top.

As Jose felt into his anger with mindful self-inquiry, an ocean of sadness about his life welled up. He realized that he hardly had any friends and that most people didn't like him. He realized that he distrusted people, and that this had its origins in his childhood. Jose had been small for his age, and kids in his neighborhood often bullied him and made fun of him because of this, leaving him feeling humiliated and inadequate. Given those experiences, it's no wonder that he didn't feel safe most of the time. As a kid, and ever since, Jose had thought the best bet was just to be as strong as possible and defend himself whenever he felt threatened. But now he had a new experience: he felt sorry for his younger self—and sorry for the person he had become as a result of those early experiences.

Jose realized that he needed to change—that he needed to have more patience with the inevitable frustrations in life, and that he needed to cultivate more acceptance and trust of others and himself, but he didn't know where to begin. When he learned loving-kindness meditation, he found the answer. Even his very first experience with this practice brought him a measure of peace that he hadn't experienced in a long time, and as he continued to practice, he discovered depths of love and connection that he hadn't imagined possible.

Mindfulness Practice: Loving-Kindness Meditation

Feeling into your heart through loving-kindness meditation will open you to what's important in life, and perhaps to what you need to work on. This meditation can elevate your heart to almost unfathomable feelings of love and may also reveal where you're holding back or stuck.

Give yourself about thirty minutes for this practice, and once you begin, bring your full, undivided attention to the practice. Read through the entire exercise before you begin. Because this practice is lengthy and specific, you may need to refer back to the text from time to time. Alternatively, you can record the instructions and listen to the recording as you practice. You can also purchase a recording of this practice at www.yourheartwideopen.com. Soon enough you'll be familiar with the practice and won't need to listen to the instructions. Also, feel free to personalize the practice. You can use the phrases provided below, but it's also fine to make up your own phrases. We've adapted the instructions for this exercise from *A Mindfulness-Based Stress Reduction Workbook*, by Bob Stahl and Elisha Goldstein (New Harbinger Publications, 2010).

Begin your practice by congratulating yourself for dedicating this time to loving-kindness meditation.

As you become present, check in with yourself and notice how you're feeling physically, mentally, and emotionally. Simply allow and acknowledge whatever you're feeling and let it be without judgment.

Gradually shift your attention to the breath, breathing normally and naturally. Focus on the nose, chest, or abdomen, being mindful of each breath, one breath at a time. As you breathe in, be aware of breathing in, and as you breathe out, be aware of breathing out. Breathing in and breathing out...

Now bring awareness into your chest and heart area and feel into your own precious and fragile life with compassion and love. If this brings up feelings of unworthiness or self-blame, know that these, too, are to be acknowledged in the open and nondiscriminating light of loving-kindness.

At times, it may seem that feelings of loving-kindness lie a long way away and you don't know how to get there. See this practice as a journey; keep walking step-by-step and know that you define the path and draw nearer to loving-kindness with each step you take. Try to feel into the qualities of loving-kindness itself, a boundless, selfless love that shines like the sun, the moon, or the stars, illuminating all beings without exception or bias.

Bring this love into your heart, skin, and bones, into your molecules and very being. May you open to deep kindness and compassion for yourself as you are.

Although it may be a struggle to feel loving toward yourself, continue to simply acknowledge your challenges and try to open to love. May you have immense self-compassion for any feelings of unworthiness, and wisdom to understand that these do not define who you are.

Take some time right now to open to each of the following phrases for a moment, allowing them to become absorbed into your being. If you would prefer to make up your own phrases, please do so.

May I open to great self-compassion.
May I open to deep reconciliation of my past with the wise
understanding that all of my past has led me to this moment.
May I hold myself gently, with mercy, kindness, and levity.
May I accept my imperfections and see that I am imperfectly
perfect just as I am.
May I be as healthy as I can be.
May I have ease in body and mind.
May I be at peace.

Now that you've begun to open yourself to loving-kindness, at some point you may quite naturally want to extend this expansive feeling outward to others. Begin by extending the feeling to those who are easy to love, such as wise and caring mentors—those who have inspired and guided you with love and wisdom. Feel into your heart with gratitude for those who have supported you, and repeat the following phrases for a couple of minutes:

May my mentors be safe from inner and outer harm.
May my mentors be happy.
May my mentors be healthy.
May my mentors be contented and at ease.
May my mentors dwell in peace.

Now gradually expand the field of loving-kindness to loved ones, such as family, friends, and community:

May my loved ones be safe from inner and outer harm.
May my loved ones be happy.
May my loved ones be healthy.
May my loved ones be contented and at ease.
May my loved ones dwell in peace.

Now further extend the field of loving-kindness to those who are neutral, whether acquaintances or strangers:

May my neutral ones be safe from inner and outer harm.
May my neutral ones be happy.
May my neutral ones be healthy.
May my neutral ones be contented and at ease.
May my neutral ones dwell in peace.

Now take some time to remember those you know who are currently living with physical pain or suffering. Bring them into your heart and extend your wishes of healing and loving-kindness to them:

May those who are suffering be safe from inner and outer harm.
May those who are suffering be happy.
May those who are suffering be healthy.
May those who are suffering be contented and at ease.
May those who are suffering dwell in peace.

Now consider extending loving-kindness even to your difficult ones or enemies. Try to neutralize any feelings of resentment, since they're so toxic to your own well-being, and understand that the hurtful actions of others often come from their fear, woundedness, and lack of awareness. Gently and slowly send loving-kindness to your difficult ones or enemies:

May my difficult ones find the gateway into their own hearts,
    gain more awareness, and transform their fear into love.
May my difficult ones be safe from inner and outer harm.
May my difficult ones be happy.
May my difficult ones be healthy.
May my difficult ones be contented and at ease.
May my difficult ones dwell in peace.

Further expand the circle of healing to all beings, building this loving-kindness to become as boundless as the sky. Begin to radiate loving-kindness outward to all living beings, sending it to all beings of the earth, the water, and the air and spreading it in all directions, throughout the entire universe:

May all beings be safe from inner and outer harm.
May all beings be happy.
May all beings be healthy.
May all beings be contented and at ease.
May all beings dwell in peace.

Gently come back to the breath and sense your entire body as you breathe in and out. Feel your entire body rising or expanding with each inhalation and descending or contracting with each exhalation. Feel your body as a single, complete organism, connected and whole. Feel the peace and loving-kindness within you and around you.

May all beings be at peace.

Take some time to write in your journal about this practice, considering these questions:

~ What was your experience of the loving-kindness meditation?

~ Did you have any obstacles, and if so, how did you work with them?

~ How can you bring more loving-kindness into your life?

Loving-kindness meditation may seem foreign to you at first, but please continue to practice it regularly. It's a practice that must be repeated to be learned. No matter how hesitant or awkward you may feel with your first steps, continued practice will create a pathway in your mind and heart that will gradually grow deeper and become your way of life, just as old pathways that numbed your mind and heart had become your way of life—except this path doesn't lead you anywhere other than right here and right now. This path is living in each breath and each heartbeat, sustaining your life and infusing it with kindness and self-compassion. Living in the moment in this way, infused with loving-kindness, allows you to let go of the past so you can live in the moment and open your heart to reconciliation and forgiveness.

What If You Don't Feel Loving?

Sometimes when you practice loving-kindness meditation, you may not feel very loving. In fact, sometimes you might experience the opposite, including strong feelings of anger, bitterness, sadness, resentment, or unworthiness. We want to assure you that this is normal. Rather than seeing such feelings as problematic or an indicator that you're somehow inadequate for not being able to do this "right," consider them to be your teacher, showing you where you're stuck or holding back and what you need to bring your attention to.

Working with these challenges can be taxing. Support yourself with compassion, and bear in mind that being aware that you're holding back allows you to move forward. If you didn't know what was holding you back, you'd be much farther away from resolving it. When you identify the causes of your pain, reconciliation may not too far behind.

Is Reconciliation Possible?

As you practice loving-kindness meditation, it may seem formidable or nearly impossible to send loving-kindness to your enemies. You may wonder why you'd even want to in the first place. At the same time, you might also realize that living with a hardened and resentful heart is a heavy load to carry and can ultimately be toxic and counterproductive to your own well-being. Psychologist Fred Luskin and colleagues at Stanford University have studied the physiological and emotional effects of forgiveness. According to Dr. Luskin, "Forgiveness can reduce stress, blood pressure, anger, depression, and hurt, and it can increase optimism, hope, compassion, and physical vitality" (2010, 127).

Ultimately, forgiveness is about making peace—making peace with what happened, and with those involved. It's typical to think of forgiveness as something you extend toward others for their wrongs against you, but this is just one aspect of it. As you work within to change your attitude and soften your heart, you'll need to cultivate three aspects of reconciliation: making peace with yourself, making peace with those you've hurt, and making with those who have hurt you. Forgiveness is really about freeing yourself.

Making Peace with Yourself

Mindfully looking into your life with kindness is liberating for many reasons, not least because it helps you see more deeply into your mistakes and learn from them. Your biggest mistakes are the places where you may learn your biggest life lessons, so rather than trying to forget or bury them, you need to understand how and why you erred. When you don't, you may have to repeat your mistakes many times before learning the lessons you need to learn. For example, you may have gotten divorced and then met someone new and wonderful, only to eventually discover that you seem to be married to the same person in a different body. Or you may repeatedly fall in love with people who eventually skip out on you and let you down, just like your father did. There are times it may seem as though you're stuck in a revolving door and doomed to make the same mistakes again and again.

But as you've learned, mindfulness can help you see the stories and habits that keep you stuck in repetitive life mistakes. It may be painful to acknowledge just how hard you've been on yourself—that you are your harshest critic and judge and that you'd never talk to anyone else the way you talk to yourself. (If you did, you probably wouldn't have any friends.) These insights may bring with them the temptation to criticize or berate yourself for being this way. As you acknowledge the events and actions that have fed into your sense of shame, guilt, deficiency, or unworthiness, hold yourself with great care and compassion. This is the key to escaping the trap of self-blame and truly freeing yourself from the cycle.

Yet as we've discussed, lack of self-compassion is pervasive, and it's no small endeavor to find your way out of the unworthy self. Making peace with yourself can be arduous. It requires patience, kindness, and insight. It's also noble and essential work that's fundamental to the healing process. You cannot make peace with others until you make peace with yourself.

As you mindfully look back at where you've been and everything that contributed to the stories you've told yourself, your behavior and automatic reactions may begin to make sense to you. You may realize, "Of course I hated myself when I was twelve. I thought I was the reason my parents got divorced. I thought I should have been a better kid." As you look back with hindsight wisdom, you'll see more clearly where you were then, why you thought and felt the way you did, and how all of this shaped the self-limiting stories you lived by for so long. As your self-compassion and your understanding of your suffering deepen, you'll feel lighter, happier, and freer.

So when practicing loving-kindness meditation, let healing and reconciliation begin inside you. May your heart open with kindness and understanding of the wounded feelings that have caused your suffering. May you hold your heart with tenderness and compassion, forgiving yourself for all the times you've been so critical of and hard on yourself. May you open to peace and reconciliation with yourself.

Making Peace with Those You've Hurt

Now that you've begun to understand and quiet your inner critic, you can use your hindsight wisdom to understand what drove you to hurt others. You'll understand where you were mentally and emotionally and why you lashed out at others in the ways you did. We've all caused pain to others, whether intentionally or not, and this can leave a bitter taste in the mouth.

Making peace with those you've hurt doesn't mean self-justification; it means taking responsibility for choices that have hurt others. This type of reconciliation involves being with things as they are and acknowledging the impact of your actions. Only then can you learn what you need to learn and let go of what you need to let go of. This type of reconciliation is a way to stop adding to the accumulated weight of negative events and memories that may fuel feelings of unworthiness. As you lay these burdens down and begin to live in the here and now, you can suspend blaming and judging of yourself and instead focus on understanding what happened or how you made mistakes, so that you can stop making them.

∼ Susan's Story

When Susan went on an intensive meditation retreat, she was beset by remorseful memories. She especially remembered and ruminated about having hurt her best friend, Erica, many years ago by telling her that the couple relationship she was in was going nowhere and asking her why she was wasting her time.

Susan shared these remorseful feelings with her mindfulness teacher, who gently suggested that Susan should feel into her shame if she was up to it, and acknowledge whatever arose for her physically, mentally, and emotionally. As Susan sat with her feelings and allowed them to surface, she met them with self-inquiry and began to gain some insight. Susan realized that her mean-spirited comments had been fueled by her own insecurity. She'd had a series of failed relationships and was worried that she would never have a long-term relationship. That had made her wonder if she wasn't good enough or lovable. She also saw that she had been jealous. These were painful, difficult insights, but because of them, Susan began to feel a deeper sense of self-compassion, and with it, a measure of acceptance and peace.

Making Peace with Those Who Have Hurt You

As with making peace with yourself for hurting others, it's important to understand that extending forgiveness to others for hurting you doesn't mean that what happened is okay. But there's an important difference: You can accept the responsibility for having hurt others, but you can't make others accept responsibility for hurting you. Perhaps this is one reason why this type of reconciliation can be so challenging. Although there are wonderful examples of people doing this, such as Pope John Paul forgiving his would-be assassin, you may think, "I'm not the pope. I'm just an ordinary person." You may wonder how you can achieve this sort of reconciliation.

The Buddha likened this to being wounded by an arrow. If that happens, your first instinct isn't to try to find out who shot it or what might have motivated them. You don't get caught up in the details of what happened and why. None of that is important until you get the arrow out of your body. In the same vein, when you live with resentments, grudges, or ill will, you are the one who's suffering. When you bring mindfulness to your body and mind and really sense how you feel when you're in a state of resentment, you'll come to know that this harboring of enmity has a toxic effect on your own health and well-being. Compare this to how your body feels when you're happy and wishing others well. This understanding is a great place to begin the work of reconciliation with others for hurting you, because it brings your own well-being into focus. While you can't change what others did—or how they are—you can change your own relationship to resentment and heal the damage that's been done in that way.

As you work on defusing resentments, you may discover that you've hurt others in ways similar to how others have hurt you, and for similar reasons, such as fear, greed, or unawareness. This can be a painful insight, but it also deepens understanding of and compassion for those who have hurt you, expanding your capacity for reconciliation and allowing you to transform and release the burden of fear and resentment. It's also useful to investigate and reflect upon the powers of reconciliation, and the following practice will help you do just that.

Mindfulness Practice: Reconciliation Meditation

As you begin to work with reconciliation in this practice, you may find that you have a hard time opening to compassion, either toward yourself or toward others. If this happens, gently and kindly acknowledge where you are. Remember, it's a practice and you're in training. As with loving-kindness meditation, these difficulties show you where you're emotionally stuck or holding back. Consider this to be good news, since seeing your challenges gives you the opportunity to work with them. As you bring the light of awareness to these stuck places, you can gradually make peace with yourself and others.

Give yourself at least twenty-five minutes for this practice. Choose a place to practice where you feel safe and at ease.

Begin by taking some time to acknowledge your aspirations to practice the reconciliation meditation. Know that this is a courageous and noble endeavor, and congratulate yourself for taking on this difficult work.

Now begin to practice mindfulness of breathing for about five minutes. Feel the sensation of the breath as it travels in and out of the nostrils, or feel the chest or belly expanding with each inhalation and contracting with each exhalation. Breathing in and out with awareness…

Now bring awareness to your chest, and feel into your heart as you breathe in and out. Reflect upon the fragility and preciousness of life—that for each of us breath is life, and when it stops, our life as we know it is over. Consider how ephemeral and short-lived each breath is, each moment is, and how nothing can stop time's passing.

As you begin to turn your focus toward reconciliation, it may be helpful to reflect upon what it feels like to hold resentments. This burden is like a thorn in your side or a stone in your shoe, and ultimately it's in your best interest to let it go. Life is so brief and so sacred, why spend it carrying these burdens? May you open to reconciliation.

Bring yourself into your own heart and open to compassion for all those times you've been judgmental or critical of yourself or filled with self-loathing. Use your wise hindsight wisdom to understand why you've hurt yourself in this way. Looking at your past self from this light now, may you open to deep compassion and love for yourself as you are. Spend at least five minutes with this reflection.

Now reflect upon times you've hurt others. Recognize and acknowledge the fears and unawareness that consumed you when you inflicted pain on others, whether intentionally or not. May you grow in deep understanding of what fueled your actions, and may there be reconciliation as your heart opens to compassion and love. Spend at least five minutes with this reflection.

Lastly, reflect upon others who have hurt you. Although it may be difficult to forgive them at first, it's important to work on neutralizing any resentment, since it directly affects your well-being. May you feel the lightness of casting off the burden of a hardened heart. Spend at least five minutes with this reflection.

Reflect that each of us is trying to find our own way—that every one of us has difficulties and uncertainties, and that no one can escape wounding others or being wounded. May all of those wounds be transformed into sites of healing. May we all find the gateway into our hearts and open to deep compassion for ourselves and others.

Conclude by returning to the breath and practicing mindfulness of the breath for five minutes. As you come to the end of this meditation, congratulate yourself for taking this time for practice. May all beings be at peace.

Take a little time to write in your journal about what you discovered in this practice. What was your experience of the reconciliation meditation? Did you encounter any challenges, and if so, how did you work with them? Consider writing out a plan to begin reconciliation with at least one person in your life.

Reconciliation is an ongoing practice, so try working with it frequently. In truth, this is the work of a lifetime. Releasing yourself from grudges is a gradual process, but in time you will become freer than you ever imagined possible.

Empathetic Joy

Empathetic joy is a wonderful quality that involves taking pleasure in another's delight. In Yiddish, the lovely word *kvell* encapsulates this quality. It means feeling happiness for others' happiness and rejoicing in their successes. Empathetic joy is the opposite of envy. All of us have had moments when we felt this way in regard to someone we care for.

You can also cultivate empathetic joy, as we'll describe below. We highly recommend it. When you're focusing on others' happiness, you aren't focusing on yourself, and this can help dispel feelings of unworthiness. In addition, empathetic joy helps you cultivate attunement and resonance with others and fosters feelings of pleasure and interconnectedness. This is a powerful antidote to the sense of isolation and disconnection that so often arise as a result of being locked into self-limiting definitions.

Mindfulness Practice: Empathetic Joy Meditation

Meditating on empathetic joy is a powerful way to connect with the timeless truth that love is meant to be shared. Give yourself about twenty minutes for this practice.

Begin by bringing awareness to the breath, being mindful of each inhalation and exhalation. Locate the spot where you feel the breath most prominently and distinctly. It could be at your nose, chest, belly, or somewhere else. Simply tune in to your breath and use it as your way to be present. Breathing in and out... Continue to practice mindful breathing for five minutes.

Now gently withdraw your attention from the breath and bring your mind and heart to someone you care about who is experiencing happiness because of something wonderful that has happened. It could be your partner being recognized for a great accomplishment at work, your child's elation over a new kitten, or a friend who has just returned from a fantastic vacation. Whatever the case may be, bring your mind to that person and allow your heart to be filled up, perhaps even overflowing, with joy for your loved one. Stay with this reflection for a few minutes.

Now pause for a minute or two and notice the joy you feel inside yourself when you feel joy for another. You may experience how wonderful it is to feel this type of joy, which brings freedom from envy and enmity.

Realizing through empathetic joy that love is meant to be shared, let your heart expand and grow, spreading this joy to others. Spend a few minutes extending empathetic joy out to other loved ones, to acquaintances, and even to strangers, being happy for their successes and happiness—and simply being happy for them that they are here in this world.

Now spend a few minutes radiating this caring joy out to all creatures great and small. May all beings experience happiness and peace in this world.

Now spend a few minutes expanding empathetic joy outward even farther, until it envelops the vast universe, and beyond. May all beings love one another and take delight in the happiness of others. May all beings be held in love and be at peace.

As you come to the end of this meditation, take a few moments to wiggle your fingers and toes, then open your eyes and feel yourself being fully present here and now.

Take a little time to write in your journal about what you experienced with this practice. What sort of physical sensations came up as you cultivated empathetic joy? What came up in your thoughts and emotions? Did you experience any challenges in doing this practice?

Practicing empathetic joy will gradually shift your limited definitions of yourself to a more expansive feeling of interconnectedness and happiness. We highly recommend that you make this practice part of your daily life.

Savoring This Journey

In this chapter we presented three mindfulness practices: loving-kindness meditation, reconciliation meditation, and empathetic joy meditation. In these practices, you extend to others the healing care and concern you developed with the self-compassion meditation in chapter 5. One aspect of reconciliation meditation is making peace with yourself—another step in your journey toward healing, self-acceptance, and wholeness. This creates a strong foundation from which you can extend loving-kindness and a spirit of reconciliation to others, healing your relationships and offering others the opportunity to experience the gifts of healing and wholeness. With time and continued practice, loving-kindness meditation and reconciliation meditation will open the door to spontaneous experiences of empathetic joy.

We recommend practicing the empathetic joy meditation frequently until it becomes an ingrained way of extending yourself to others. Practice reconciliation anytime you feel your heart hardening against yourself or others. Consider making loving-kindness meditation a lifelong practice, as it can foster self-compassion, dissolve feelings of separateness, and help you cultivate a spirit of reconciliation and empathetic joy.

Chapter 7

~

Becoming Real

There was a time when meadow, grove, and stream,
The earth, and every common sight,
To me did seem
Apparelled in celestial light,
The glory and the freshness of a dream.

—William Wordsworth

The joy of becoming real is discovering our liveliness and the freshness and uniqueness of each new moment. We come home to a wholeness and sense of belonging in the world that's always been with us, even if we weren't aware of it. In this chapter we'll explore ways we can help ourselves and one another awaken to the exquisite vividness of each moment.

This type of awakening is fundamental to Buddhism. Indeed, the word "Buddha" means "one who is awake," particularly in the sense of understanding the causes of suffering and how to end it. The Buddha realized that the fundamental cause of suffering is identifying with a self that feels separate from everyone and everything else. Einstein also acknowledged this fundamental truth in a letter quoted in the *New York Post* (1972): "We experience ourselves, our thoughts and feelings, as something separate from the rest—a kind of optical delusion of consciousness. This delusion is a kind of prison for us, restricting us to our personal desires and to affection for a few persons nearest us."

The delusion of a separate self is the source of lust, anger, and the many permutations of these forces that create so much anguish in our lives. In his letter to the *Post*, Einstein went on to say, "Our task must be to free ourselves from this prison by widening our circle of compassion to embrace all living creatures and the whole of nature in its beauty" (1972). This too reflects Buddhist psychology, which maintains that as we widen our circle of loving-kindness and mindfulness, we can free ourselves from the delusions of the conditioned mind and realize a wholeness and completeness within ourselves and all things. This is the pathway to awakening to a much larger sense of who you are.

Becoming Who You Are

A Sri Lankan meditation master offered a simple explanation of the essence of Buddhism to former Buddhist monk Jack Kornfield: Laughing, the master said, "No self, no problem" (Kornfield 1993, 203). You may ask, "If I have no self, then who am I?" That's a good question, and one that has been asked for millennia in many religions and spiritual paths. It's a central question of philosophy and psychology as well, and also a very hard question to answer with concepts. As soon as you attach concepts to the self, you risk setting it apart from everything and everyone else. The self cannot be known in a concept; it's a here-and-now experience that exists only in the immediacy of each moment. It's not a thing; it's an experience. You get a sense of this immediacy when you wonder, "Who is asking these questions about self? Who is speaking words with my mouth, or listening with my ears?" There is someone motivating your actions and experiencing your senses. But consider: These are all immediate experiences that exist only in the experiencing.

We all live only in this moment. We don't live, or see, or take action in any other moment.

In previous chapters, we discussed how all of us become identified with a narrative-based self. You've learned mindfulness skills that can help you recognize and disidentify from the self you've created. In turn, the meditative awareness of mindfulness grows even as you attend to the conditioned self with curiosity and detachment. As you witness thoughts and emotions coming and going, you become more the witnessing than the stories being witnessed. In this way, mindfulness can become more than what you do; it can become a way of life and a way of being with others in the world. It can become who you are. So it is that Mahatma Gandhi could say, "My life is my message" (Ghose 1991, 386). Gandhi is also reported to have said, "We must be the change we wish to see" (Einhorn 1991, 71). Similarly, we might say that being real is to live the truth, love, wisdom, and compassion we want to see in the world.

Moments of Awakening

Most of us have had moments of awakening in unlikely places and times, such as airports or street corners, as well as in more likely places, like extended meditation retreats or while sitting by a mountain lake. In these moments, we suddenly have access to a natural wisdom that feels like it's always been within us. Yet we typically also discover how quickly we can be lulled back into operating on autopilot, losing touch with the wisdom and perspective we'd discovered. You may leave a retreat feeling like you're living within a new clarity and understanding, only to discover that, shortly after returning to daily life and the social world, you're already lost in some ego trip or another. We all discover soon enough that the conditioned self doesn't vanish as we awaken. It's always present to a greater or lesser degree and must simply become a part of our richness as we navigate in the world. The key is to become familiar with the distortions of your conditioned self and learn to recognize when you fall under its spell.

Barry, a longtime student of mindfulness, told a story that illustrates how easily we can fall back into our delusions and ingrained behaviors. He had returned from a weekend meditation retreat just a few days prior. Finding himself in a bad mood, he decided to take a walk. Seeing him leave their yard, his wife called from the kitchen window, "Where are you going, honey?" His response leapt from his mouth like a toad: "I'm going down to the river to club rats!" he shot back. She came running from the front door; "Are you all right?" she asked, knowing full well that there was no river nearby and no rats, and that even if there were, he would never do such a thing. Barry realized what had happened and apologized: "I'm sorry, honey, I'm feeling really frustrated right now and was going for a walk. I'm sorry for saying that. I got you temporarily confused with my mother—again."

Even as your mindfulness practice grows, you may become identified with a small, contracted self from time to time and speak or act from this unconscious place. Mindfulness (and sometimes your loved ones or friends) can help you notice when you've fallen into the delusions of the conditioned self again. Simply acknowledge what has happened with self-compassion and without blame, then return to the here and now and live from your wholeness and clarity. It's just like in formal mindfulness practice: The moment you notice you're lost, you're no longer lost. The moment you recognize that you weren't here, you're here again.

Perhaps this is one of the reasons why beginner's mind is such an important aspect of mindfulness: The path to awakening involves beginning again innumerable times—sometimes hundreds of times in just one meditation practice. Yet repetition is a time-honored spiritual practice, and we wake up a little more each time. This is why becoming real often takes a long time. Beginning again is how we progress and gradually come to live and speak the truth of our lives. Every time we return to mindfulness and compassion, these faculties are strengthened, and eventually they become how we progress and express ourselves. In time, mindfulness and compassion may become a way of life.

Personality Patterns

Becoming real can free you from habits of personality that you've come to identify with. When you speak from a wide-open heart, you aren't constrained by unconscious ways of expressing yourself. As discussed in chapter 1, unmet needs can drive us to create maladaptive personality patterns when we're very young. In time, these patterns become automatic and we manifest them without being aware that we're doing so. What began as an effort to get our needs met can become dysfunctional and color many of our interpersonal relationships with the hues of an injured heart. One interesting way of looking at and understanding these personality patterns is through schemas, discussed in depth in psychotherapist Tara Bennett-Goleman's book *Emotional Alchemy* (2001). She identifies ten major schemas, each of which has many variations, and she illuminates the emotional hues of each schema. Most of us have one or two of these as primary schemas in our lives (Bennett-Goleman 2001):

~ **Subjugation** is putting others' wishes and needs ahead of your own in order to be acceptable. In this pattern you may chronically depreciate yourself and feel as though you don't have enough value to lead others, so you must follow and accommodate what others want.

~ **Perfectionism** is an effort to win the attention and approval you crave by doing everything just right. This pattern ensures you will always be engaged in critically evaluating your performance or appearance. The internal critic is always at work and pushing you.

~ **Fear of abandonment** manifests as pervasive insecurity in relationships. If this schema applies to you, it matters little what your spouse or lover or close friends tell you. Their care and assurances seem hollow, and you live in fear of being left alone.

~ **Fragility** shows up as feeling fearful in relatively safe situations and inflating relatively minor events to catastrophic proportions. With this schema, you're afraid you could break easily.

~ **Unlovability** is the fear that you're fundamentally flawed or defective and therefore aren't lovable. With this pattern, you may feel that there's something missing or so wrong with you that others cannot love you.

~ **Grandiosity** is the sense that you deserve special treatment. Outwardly, this is the mirror opposite of the unlovability pattern, but the inner attitude is the same: Because you feel flawed, you behave in grandiose ways to disprove or deflect the negative opinions you believe others have.

~ **Emotional deprivation** manifests as the feeling that you'll never have your emotional needs met. When caught in this pattern, it doesn't matter how sensitive and nurturing your friends and partners are; you'll still believe that you'll always be emotionally frustrated.

~ **Social exclusion** is a pattern that involves having a pervasive sense that you just don't belong with others. If you're under the effect of this schema, you'll feel alienated and think of yourself as an ugly duckling or black sheep.

~ **Skepticism** shows up as paranoia and mistrust of others. In this pattern, you feel suspicious of everyone and believe that no one is trustworthy.

~ **The failure complex** is a sense of being deficient and never succeeding, no matter what you actually achieve. This can be a self-fulfilling prophesy. Why bother trying if you will always fail anyway?

One thing all schemas have in common is that they keep us trapped in conditioned habits of mind that ultimately interfere with deep connectedness with ourselves and others, and this makes loving intimacy impossible. In addition, they're all built on a faulty assumption: that there's something wrong with you, and if you can somehow correct it, you'll get the fulfillment or safety you crave. But this is the trap of self-improvement we discussed in chapter 5, and it will only keep you stuck in a feeling of deficiency. So what's the answer? It's helpful to learn to recognize your schemas. By seeing and even befriending them, you can keep yourself from falling under their spell.

Recognizing your schemas can also help you understand why you might tend to repeat certain patterns in relationships. For example, if you tend to choose partners who are abusive, it may be an unconscious effort to reenact early traumatic experiences so you can master them. And though it may seem counterintuitive, meeting people who seem to offer the opportunity to repeat these disastrous relationship patterns is usually exciting. This is why people who long for emotional connectedness so often end up getting married to people who are cold and aloof. But all is not lost. There's a way to transform these relationship patterns: mindfully witnessing the stories that drive them and compassionately embracing the feelings within them. The next exercise will help you do just that.

Exercise: Recognizing Your Schemas

This exercise will help you identify any schemas that may be involved in limiting self-conceptions and habitual patterns of relating to others.

Over the next week, pay attention to yourself in relationships with those who are important to you, to see if you can identify your habitual schemas, using the list above as a guide. In your journal, make daily notes about the times and places you noticed schema patterns at work. Also note whom you were with and the circumstances you were in. In each instance, see if you can figure out what purpose your schema meant to serve, and record that in your journal as well.

We recommend that you also enlist the assistance of a trusted friend or family member as you investigate your schemas. Others can often see our schemas more clearly than we can. Go over the list of schemas together and see if the other person recognizes the same schema patterns in you that you have. Then take some time to write in your journal about what you discover in these conversations.

After listing and exploring your schemas, spend a little time with each of them, investigating whether you can determine what sort of childhood experiences might have led to their creation. Again, spend some time writing in your journal about what comes up for you.

Finally, investigate how well your schemas are working for you. Are these patterns that you want to maintain in your life and relationships? What sort of emotions come up for you when you fall into the grip of each schema? If you don't want to maintain these patterns, how can you begin to break free of them? Are there signals that can alert you that you're beginning to fall into a particular schema? Again, take some time to write in your journal about what you've learned about yourself here.

You can return to this exercise anytime to further investigate any schema patterns you notice.

Accepting Yourself as You Are

As long as you're swept up in a narrative-based sense of self and all of the limitations and suffering that entails, you can neither find nor heal your wounded heart, and therefore you remain a prisoner of your childhood. Self-concepts like unworthiness and inadequacy often serve as a distraction from the feelings the story conceals. To live with your heart wide open, you must find, feel, and accept all of your feelings.

Your way of experiencing emotions will change as you learn to be in them and let them come and go without thinking they define you. Rather than thinking, "I'm always so stupid and out of control. Why do I have to be like this?" you might look at it more like "I'm feeling ashamed of what I did, and it hurts." Instead of wondering, "Why do I have to be such an angry person?" you might think, "Wow, I'm really feeling angry. It hurt my feelings when she said that." As you increasingly live in the immediacy-based self, you'll learn to be with your emotions in a more open and accepting way, without criticizing yourself or believing that your emotions represent character flaws that affirm some ingrained self-story.

You don't have to look far to find the feelings you need to feel. Whether you just started meditating with the practices in this book or have been sitting for many years, you've probably noticed that the thoughts and emotions you have the most difficulty with can and often do arise and fill your mind during meditation practice. Generally, this is the opposite of the experience you were looking for! This is why meditation is sometimes called a "shit accelerator." Whether you want them or not, sooner or later you discover feelings that were squelched for one reason or another. Perhaps you repressed them because you didn't have a way to cope with them in the situations where they first came up. Maybe you don't show your anger now because your parents couldn't tolerate your anger. Or maybe you don't initiate sex because you don't feel worthy enough to believe someone would want you.

Emotions come to the surface as you feel deeply into the stories you've been hiding in. This means that these stories can become beneficial if you work with them mindfully. This may seem to contradict much of what we've been teaching about how stories beguile us into the delusion of a fixed and stable self, but if you look into your stories with the compassionate curiosity of mindfulness, you'll find that they carry within them repressed feelings that may hold a great deal of value for you. Embracing these feelings will liberate you from the confines of self these stories weave. The key is to feel the feelings and notice their expression in your body without getting caught up in the identity the stories create. Don't buy into them; listen to them with your heart and turn toward the deeper feelings hidden within them. As you grow in tolerance and acceptance of your emotions, you'll gradually be able to feel more deeply into the feelings that your stories have concealed. And as you open to accept what you feel, you'll discover that even a painful story is like a treasure chest, holding within it your heart of hearts.

The Value of Radical Acceptance

A huge part of meditation practice is learning to say yes to what is— learning to relax and just let things happen as they will in your mind and body. This is sometimes called *radical acceptance* (Brach 2004). You might think of it as softening around what comes up for you, rather than contracting. This is particularly important when you discover that many of your harshest judgments are of yourself. This isn't unusual; when we turn inward, many of us find that we're harder on ourselves than anyone else is, or than we are with anyone else. See if you can soften around these self-judgments, and notice whether doing so helps you grow in self-acceptance. You can learn to let everything be, both within yourself and in the world around you. You can learn to be just as you are and to stop wanting to be somehow different. In this way, you may also release yourself from the subtle aggression of self-improvement.

In working with aversive emotions, it's helpful to sometimes shift from the intensity of the emotion and focus on the physical sensations connected to it. You may notice that fear expresses itself differently in your body than shame or anxiety. See if you can work with unpleasant emotions by softening around the sensations connected to them. The immediacy of your sensory experience will help you remain grounded in the moment. Even with very difficult emotions like shame, fear, or grief, you can begin defusing their explosive charge and gradually integrate them into your life by grounding your awareness in the body as these emotions arise.

Know that radical acceptance doesn't mean you're okay with terrible things that have happened to you or abusive situations or relationships you may currently be coping with. It simply means you acknowledge that whatever happened has happened. And, as we noted before, if you're working with trauma, it's wise and skillful to enlist the aid of a trusted teacher or therapist to help you in this process.

Habits of reactive distancing and clinging are deeply ingrained in the conditioned self and can happen automatically and without thought. When you notice that you've suddenly distanced yourself from or are clinging to a thought or feeling, this is a moment to practice radical acceptance.

Mindfulness Practice: Radical Acceptance

The intention of all mindfulness practice is to take everything off of automatic—to learn to respond rather than react to whatever you encounter. But if you're unable to accept your experience for what it is, you'll continue to resist it and react to it. Learning to be with and accept things as they are is a key to the mindful path, and a powerful way to live with your heart wide open. Give yourself about thirty minutes for this practice of radical acceptance.

Begin by practicing mindful breathing for at least ten minutes. Let your breath come and go as it will, and use the sensations of breathing as your way to be present.

Next, open your awareness to attend to the thoughts and emotions that come up for you. Particularly attend to thoughts or emotions that you experience as painful or aversive—things you fear, hate, or wish to avoid. For the next ten minutes, notice what you resist and your reactions as these thoughts and feelings come up.

Feel into and acknowledge each of these unpleasant thoughts and emotions as simply as possible; for example, "fear that no one will love me," "fear of being alone," or "hatred of my fat body." Make space for these feelings with an attitude of acceptance and allowing. If it's helpful, say yes to each of these thoughts and feelings and then let them be. "I was so mean." "Yes." "I was so defensive." "Yes." "I was so seductive." "Yes." Recognize that things are as they are. Something happened or didn't happen. Simply let everything be and say yes to it. As you attend to these thoughts and feelings, use your breath as a way to anchor yourself in the present moment.

When you're ready, recenter in the body and turn the whole of your attention to the sensations of the breath coming and going. Acknowledge that the thoughts and emotions you were having are now past and that you can let them be. They were sometimes pleasant and sometimes unpleasant, but they were all impermanent events. Spend another ten minutes just attending to the breath and returning to the felt sense of the breath every time you notice you've left it.

Take a little time to write in your journal about your radical acceptance practice. Acknowledge and record any particular patterns that emerged as you investigated unpleasant thoughts and feelings; for example, lots of self blame for unrealistic expectations, judgments that sound a lot like the things your parents said to you when they were drinking, or shame that follows closely on the heels of a craving for reassurance and acceptance from someone you're attracted to. Take note of those things you had a particularly difficult time saying yes to.

Ego Is a Good Thing

With all of the time and intention we've invested in helping you dis-identify from the narrative-based self and live in the here and now, you may think we believe ego is a bad thing and you have to get rid of it. We want to clarify that this isn't our message—and that it isn't even possible. Actually, the ego is a good servant, but it's a disastrous master. As you grow in mindful awareness, you'll come to understand the workings of your ego and the stories that comprise your narrative-based self. The more you grow in this understanding, the easier it will be to take these stories and the ego itself lightly. At a retreat we attended a few years ago, author and meditation teacher Wes Nisker offered a quip from Ram Dass that expresses this perfectly. When asked how his lifetime of meditation had affected idiosyncrasies of his personality, Ram Dass replied, "Oh, I don't take my personality so seriously anymore. I consider it more as a pet now."

The fact is, you need to have a healthy ego to get free of the delusions your ego spins. You need the ego strengths of tolerance, acceptance, compassion, forgiveness, and emotional self-regulation to help you recognize and free yourself from the constricted sense of self that has created so much suffering in your life. No one gets rid of the ego—it's essential to our navigation in this world. But hopefully we will all grow more skillful in using it and not being used by it. Seeing your ego more as a tool and less as your identity will help you free yourself from stories that constrict and limit your life, allowing you to discover more authentic and liberating elements in your life story. And from a more expansive point of view, you may recognize that some of the troublesome parts of your story have been necessary for you to become who you are in your fullness. They may also be instrumental in helping others who struggle with similar life issues. In this way, you can use the stories that once trapped you to serve your awakening and the awakening of others.

Being Truthful with Yourself

Mindfulness enables us to see the qualities of ego and personality that have spurred us to begin this practice in the first place: the cravings and aversions, the attachments and delusions, the things we hate about ourselves or others—all of the things that create so much suffering in our lives. But now you know that seeing these things isn't the same as identifying with them, and that as disturbing as they might be, witnessing these internal experiences and letting them be is your key to freedom. It's what enables you to recognize these habits of mind and disidentify from the conditioned self.

In time, the conditioned self no longer rules your life; it becomes just another aspect of who you are. You won't take it so seriously anymore. In fact, it can even be something to chuckle at from time to time. As this self becomes less prominent, so do the attachments and sufferings associated with it, and this creates more space for your immediacy-based self to flourish. Along the way, you'll notice that your story is a lot like everyone else's story and that you aren't so alone in the world. All human beings have to find a way to cope with suffering in their lives. When you live with your heart wide open to this realization, you discover a greater connectedness with and compassion for everyone and everything—including yourself. In this way, the skills of mindfulness and self-inquiry allow you to investigate and accept all of your authentic feelings and the truth of your unique history. In opening to these feelings, you may find your way home to yourself with truthfulness and love.

∼ Brittany's Story

As Brittany started watching her mind at work during a meditation retreat, she was horrified to discover how judgmental of others she was. The way a man blew his nose made him an object of her contempt for half an hour. The amount of food a woman took at lunch disgusted her and filled her mind with criticism throughout her meal. In her third day of practice, she herself became the object of her judgments and spent most of the day condemning herself for being such a judgmental person. The more she noticed these things, the more she suffered. She decided to leave the retreat, but then found an opportunity to discuss her self-made hell with a teacher, who helped her see that this misery of mind wasn't happening because she was meditating—it was happening all the time in her day-to-day life. She had simply begun to notice it because she was meditating. Brittany decided to stay and work with this old habit with more acceptance and compassion.

At the suggestion of the teacher, Brittany invested herself in the AWARE practice for the rest of the retreat. Each day, she found herself acknowledging judgments hundreds of times. Each time, she reoriented to compassionate awareness and letting be. She took this practice home and decided to live within it, as a new way of being in the world. Over the next couple of months, the judgments remained almost as prolific as ever, but at least she wasn't taking them so seriously.

Being Truthful with Others

Paying attention to yourself in interpersonal relationships can be very revealing, often in embarrassing ways. Often, who you are when you're with others doesn't match up with who you are when you're alone. Yet, ultimately, being real means being who you are all the time, including when you're with others. This is usually much easier said than done. We tend to take our fear of others' opinions too much to heart. Sometimes it can be helpful to consider the advice of financier and statesman Bernard Baruch: "Those who matter don't mind, and those who mind don't matter" (Cerf 1948, 249).

Still, it can be hard to be real in your interpersonal relationships, especially when you're operating on autopilot. As you travel the path of mindfulness and self-inquiry, it's helpful to have at least one friend whom you're willing to speak your truth to, and who can respond to you with truth as well (in a good way, even if you don't like hearing it at first). Such a friend can inspire you, comfort you, and remind you why you even began to meditate. When you've gotten lost in your conditioned self again, such a friend may be able to help you reclaim your mindfulness. And when those near and dear to you have lost their way, you may be able to help them, in turn. At this level of sharing, it's especially important to bring the skills of mindfulness, loving-kindness, and compassion into speaking truth to one another.

Friendship is of vital importance on this pathway of awakening. We need the friendship of others if we are to grow and fully realize the truth and love we find in our hearts. Each of us discovers different things along the way, and by sharing them, we can all contribute to one anothers' awakening.

We need one another in many other ways, as well. We discover who we are in how we're reflected in the eyes of those who understand, accept, and support us. We become real in their love. A passage from the story *The Velveteen Rabbit* illustrates this in a delightfully whimsical way (Williams 1922, 4-5):

> "What is *Real*?" asked the Rabbit one day... "Does it mean having things that buzz inside you and a stick-out handle?"
>
> "Real isn't how you are made," said the Skin Horse. "It's a thing that happens to you. When a child loves you for a long, long time, not just to play with, but *really* loves you, then you become Real."
>
> "Does it hurt?" asked the Rabbit.
>
> "Sometimes," said the Skin Horse, for he was always truthful. "When you are Real you don't mind being hurt."
>
> "Does it happen all at once, like being wound up," he asked, "or bit by bit?"
>
> "It doesn't happen all at once," said the Skin Horse. "You become. It takes a long time. That's why it doesn't happen often to people who break easily, or have sharp edges, or who have to be carefully kept. Generally, by the time you are Real, most of your hair has been loved off, and your eyes drop out and

you get loose in the joints and very shabby. But these things don't matter at all, because once you are Real you can't be ugly, except to people who don't understand… Once you are Real you can't become unreal again. It lasts for always."

In childhood, we might find ourselves in how we're reflected in a loving parent's eyes. As adults, we might find this sort of clear reflection from a supportive spouse, a trusted friend, or a therapist. In Buddhism we may find truth speaking with a teacher or in the *sangha*, the spiritual friendship of a community of fellow practitioners. In Christianity this kind of healing community is called fellowship; in Hinduism, it's *satsang*, or company of truth; and in Sufism it's *sohbet*. Every healing and spiritual path acknowledges the value of interpersonal relationships where we can be authentic, speak our truth, and access our genuine feelings.

A natural vitality emerges when we acknowledge and accept feelings we swallowed up in childhood and have kept hidden ever since. And being in relationships where we can feel and speak these feelings makes us feel even more real and alive. Martin Luther King Jr. put it well: "I believe that unarmed truth and unconditional love will have the final word in reality" (1992, 110).

What Does It Mean to Become Real?

Throughout this book we've discussed how mindfulness can help you move outside your normal processes of self-referencing to discover a larger sense of who you are. When you are no longer identified with limiting self-stories, you'll discover a new freedom, and you never have to return to who you used to be. This enlargement of self is a kind of transcendence. Literally, the "trance ends," and you are no longer identified with a story of a separate self that feels disconnected from everyone else. You are no longer contracted within self-centered, judgmental self-definitions and endless concerns about whether you're somehow deficient. As that old story falls away, your heart can open wide to discover your place in a much larger story—your place in the family of all beings and all of nature. Becoming real means awakening to your innate wholeness and interconnectedness.

Becoming real takes a long time, and sometimes it hurts. By the time you're real, you can be pretty beat-up, old, and shabby (as the Skin Horse in *The Velveteen Rabbit* said). Along the way, most of us endure many interpersonal disasters, humiliations, and enormous life problems. That's why becoming real doesn't happen to people who are too fragile. Meditation isn't for the faint of heart. Learning to disidentify from the narrative-based self is often arduous and overwhelming. After a while, though, it becomes less upsetting or disruptive to catch yourself being possessed by those old stories again, and it may even be a little humorous.

Of course, some of the ways in which we can be possessed by our stories aren't at all humorous. When they are harmful to ourselves or others, as in the case of aggression, sexual misconduct, and other destructive or addictive behaviors, a serious response is called for. Either way, the key is mindful awareness. Notice when you're slipping into autopilot mode, and when you see this happening, choose to live more deliberately. Be present. Stay in touch with your sense of loving-kindness and compassion and use these strengths to dissolve every destructive habitual pattern of behavior. Anytime you feel compelled to do something impulsively or find yourself reacting in automatic ways, be very suspicious. Habitual behaviors that arise from old stories are often driven by craving or fear. When you pause before responding, you can investigate the source of these automatic reactions with mindful self-inquiry: Where is this coming from? Does it arise out of fear, anger, or desire? Could this action hurt anyone? Do you really have to act on this feeling right now?

Mindfulness Practice: Interpersonal Inquiry

A friend of ours has a very interesting greeting on his answering machine: "Who are you, and what do you want?" Reportedly, there is often a long silence before his callers respond. These are deep questions and worthy of deep personal inquiry. One powerful way of exploring these questions is through the following practice of mindful interpersonal inquiry.

Choose someone to share this practice with whom you feel close to and can trust. This practice includes mindful breathing. If need be, explain mindful breathing to your partner before beginning. You might even practice mindful breathing together a few times before trying the lengthier, more involved practice below. Once you're ready to begin practicing interpersonal inquiry, plan two sessions, each about an hour and fifteen minutes in duration. You can do the two sessions on the same day or on separate days. It would be useful to have a timer that can sound fifteen-minute intervals so that you can be fully engaged in the practice without having to watch a clock. Before beginning, read through the practice below to get an idea of what's involved, and decide who will inquire first before you start.

First Practice: Who Are You?

Sit directly across from your partner and practice mindful breathing for fifteen minutes.

When the fifteen minutes is up, make eye contact and then begin the inquiry. The inquirer asks, "Who are you?" After receiving a response, the inquirer pauses for a few moments and then asks the question once again. Continue this practice for fifteen minutes, then sit in silence for a few minutes.

Switch roles and repeat the process.

Reflect on what came up for you in the inquiry for five minutes, and then meditate on the breath in silence for ten minutes. At the end of the silent meditation, give each other five minutes to talk about this experience.

Second Practice: What Do You Want?

Once again, sit directly across from your partner and practice mindful breathing for fifteen minutes.

When the fifteen minutes is up, make eye contact and then begin the inquiry. The inquirer asks, "What do you want?" After receiving a response, the inquirer pauses for a few moments and then asks the question once again. Continue this practice for fifteen minutes, then sit in silence for a few minutes.

Switch roles and repeat the process.

Reflect on what came up for you in the inquiry for five minutes, and then meditate on the breath in silence for ten minutes. At the end of the silent meditation, give each other five minutes to talk about this experience.

These questions and variations on the theme can be very revealing in regard to your conditioned self and the extent to which you're identified with it. Other questions to consider include "What role do you tend to play in intimate relationships?" "What role do you play in your work or profession?" "What role do you play as a parent?" "What role do you play when you're with your parents?" "What role do you play as a neighbor?" "What role do you play as a customer?" Get creative; there are many ways to work with a partner to explore who you are and how you are. A continuing dialogue between you and your meditation partner can help you discover many things about yourself that you might not recognize on your own. Return to this practice again and again to see what you discover.

This practice will be much richer when you work with a partner you can share your truth deeply with. However, it may be that you currently don't have someone with whom you can dive into this kind of exchange. However, you can still explore these questions as a writing practice in your journal. Create the same circumstances for yourself as if you were working with a partner, setting a timer and writing, from the immediacy of your experience, whatever these questions bring up for you. Because writing takes longer than speaking, give yourself more time for each inquiry.

Love as a Way of Being

In Islamic tradition, it's said that the divine motivation for creation sprang from the desire to be known, with God reportedly saying, "I was a hidden treasure. I longed to be known, so I created the world that I might be known" (Frager and Fadiman 1999, 92). Sometimes we sense that there's much more to being human than we have allowed ourselves to know. We sense that there's a deep internal wellspring of wisdom, compassion, and love, and that there's something we are supposed to do with it. We come to know these treasures in the expression of them. A poem by Rumi expresses this beautifully (1997, 31):

> Today, like every other day, we wake up empty
> and frightened. Don't open the door to the study
> and begin reading. Take down a musical instrument.
> Let the beauty we love be what we do.
> There are hundreds of ways to kneel and kiss the ground.

We love Rumi (and gifted translator Coleman Barks) because he speaks from a wide-open heart so eloquently. We can find the treasures of peace, loving-kindness, and gentleness within ourselves when we let the beauty we love be what we do. If you want to learn about love, love this breath—this expression of life as it's happening in your body. Do it now. Don't just ponder the concept—really do it. Close your eyes and love this breath as you are feeling it. Love isn't what you think. It's what you do; it's a way of being in the world. Likewise, mindfulness and compassion aren't just something to read about; these are ways to be. As you find the feelings that have lain buried and hidden within your heart and embrace them, you may come to know and love the heart that has always held them. You discover who you are and always have been as you emerge from who you are not and never were. As the flower falls away, a delicious fruit appears. As you let go of the caterpillar body of your story, you are given wings. You become who you are. You become real. This is why so many prophets and ecstatic poets speak of the need to die before you can be reborn.

Imagine being at sea on a calm night, your ship gliding through the stillness. The stars are shining as bright in the mirror of the water as they are in the sky, and you cannot find a line between what is above and what is below. Suspended here, you become still, floating some-where between a vastness below and another above. Your heart fills with love. You search for the line that separates you from everything else. It isn't there, and you too become part of the vastness.

If you want to live with your heart wide open, become like a river that endlessly joins with the sea. This is what it means to become real through love: allowing love to transform you so greatly that you, like the river, become infinite as you give yourself completely and endlessly to love and compassion—an embodied presence that embraces everyone and everything as part of one great whole.

Savoring This Journey

In this chapter we presented two mindfulness practices: radical acceptance and interpersonal inquiry. Radical acceptance is an extension of the work you began with mindful self-inquiry. It brings the focused awareness of mindfulness to those thoughts and feelings that seem most painful and aversive. Yet at this stage in your mindful journey, you've honed and developed many aspects of mindfulness, including noting, cultivating spaciousness, self-compassion, and reconciliation. This will help you extend radical acceptance to even these most difficult thoughts and emotions. This is the key to equanimity, and essential to continuing to live with your heart wide open, no matter what circumstances life may bring you. We recommend that you practice radical acceptance frequently in a formal way until it feels natural to you. Then you can more easily bring this perspective to your day-to-day life.

Interpersonal inquiry is a way of broadening your mindfulness practice to include others. If you find others who are interested in practicing together with you in this way, take advantage of this opportunity on a regular basis.

Chapter 8

~

Awakening to Wisdom and Compassion

Love has befriended Hafiz so completely
It has turned to ash and freed me
Of every concept and image
My mind has ever known.

—Hafiz

It is possible to break free from the grip of unworthiness, inadequacy, and shame. Hopefully everything you've learned in this book and in your mindfulness practice has assured you of that. There will be times when you'll slip into autopilot mode and once again get caught in your story, but remember, the moment you realize you aren't present, you're present once again. The moment you become aware that you're trapped by your thoughts or emotions, you can begin to free yourself.

Mindfulness is the place where you can see clearly and make intelligent choices—choices informed by the present moment, not your past or an imagined future. There is nothing like the present moment, and the good news is, it's with you every moment—wherever you are. Every moment is an opportunity to begin again. So no matter how many times you aren't present, you can become present once again with tender mercy and compassion.

In the previous chapter we talked about becoming real. As you continue to work with all of the mindfulness and compassion practices you've learned in this book, you'll increasingly break free from the confines of the narrative-based self. As you become more mindful and increasingly operate from the immediacy-based self, you can live more spaciously. This jewel of awakening is your birthright; it's something that exists within all of us. The doorway is in your heart. There's no need to look outside; everything you need to know is inside you—perhaps it just needs to be discovered. Finding yourself and becoming real isn't unlike Michelangelo chiseling a block of marble to reveal David standing right inside it.

Remember, you weren't born "bad" or somehow deficient. There truly is more right with you than there is wrong with you, and it isn't your fault that somewhere along the way you lost your sovereignty.

This being the final chapter, we want to offer you a grand finale. Don't think of the work in this chapter as the conclusion to the book or the end of this process and path; rather, it's the next step in the journey of your lifetime, and another step to greater freedom. We feel there is no work more noble than inner work on oneself. The work you do to heal yourself also heals the world. Bringing peace to the world begins inside you and within every one of us. In this chapter we'll explore ways you can foster deeper mindfulness, wisdom, and compassion so that you can extend the gifts within you to the world.

The Second Noble Truth

Buddhist psychology speaks of four primary principles—the Four Noble Truths—as being integral to freeing ourselves from the confines of a limited self-concept. The first is that pain is inevitable. Each of us has to deal with difficult situations, and no one can escape from aging, illness, death, or separation. The second is that suffering is caused by craving or grasping, which are fueled by ignorance. The third is that there is a way out of suffering, through relinquishing our grasping and ignorance. The fourth is an elaboration on the path to freedom from suffering. Known as the Noble Eightfold Path, it describes eight life principles that can help us free ourselves from suffering, attachment, and the confines of the narrative-based self.

Let's take a deeper look at the second principle, the cause of suffering, since this is what lies at the root of the dilemma this book addresses. Ajahn Amaro offered an insightful translation of this principle: "This is the noble truth of the cause of suffering: it is craving that is compelling, intoxicating—which causes us to be born into things again and again, ever seeking delight now here, now there, namely craving for sensual delight, the craving to be something, and the craving to feel nothing" (2010).

This type of intoxicating grasping and aversion fuels the narrative-based self. When we're either looking for more or pushing away what's here, we're rarely contented, leading to a life of perennial dissatisfaction. The truth is, everything is impermanent, so no matter how gratifying anything is, it won't last.

Working with Your Demons

We've devoted a lot of discussion to how the narrative-based self is constructed. And while you can't be held responsible for the early childhood events that led to creation of your story, you can choose how to respond in the here and now. A powerful turning point in your relationship to your narrative-based self occurs when you begin to take responsibility for your actions, and thereby for your own happiness or sadness. Understanding and appreciating how much your actions contribute to the construction of the narrative-based self can be immensely liberating, but getting there can be a frightening excursion. You may recognize that you have to change your ways, and the conditioned self doesn't like that.

You may have noticed that sometimes you'd rather live in a dysfunctional way than take the risk of trying something new. Often, we don't find the willingness to change until the suffering in our lives becomes great enough. Yet stepping into the unknown is a wonderful way of discovering more freedom. You must face your fears to find and open your heart. This isn't a new concept; it's been around for millennia in various traditions, and it was key in the enlightenment of Siddhartha Gautama, who became known as the Buddha, or the Awakened One. This enlightenment or awakening occurred through the overcoming of grasping, aversion, and unawareness of his conditioned self.

It is said that during the night of his enlightenment, Siddhartha was visited and tempted by Mara, who could be considered a manifestation of the psychological aspects of greed, hatred, and ignorance— those voices you hear inside your head that lead to grasping, aversion, and delusion and create feelings of inadequacy, shame, and unworthiness. They speak to you when you say to yourself, "I'll never be good enough," "I don't even know where to begin," or any of the self-defeating messages you tell yourself when you're trapped within the confines of the narrative-based self.

Throughout the night of the Buddha's awakening, Mara pounded him with armies of fear and lustful temptation in an attempt to distract him from his quest, but every time Mara attacked, Siddhartha didn't react. Instead, he simply said, "I see you, Mara." His clear seeing and choice not to react stripped Mara of any power to influence him, releasing Mara's clasp on his mind and heart.

After his long vigil that night, Siddhartha developed deep insight into the Four Noble Truths (suffering, its cause, its cessation, and the eightfold path to freedom) and became known as the Buddha, or the Awakened One. He saw through his conditioned self and attained the unconditioned self, or enlightenment. In the same way, you too can learn to sit with your own manifestations of grasping, aversion, and ignorance and begin to name and acknowledge them. Begin to say, "I see you, Mara," to your desires, judgments, and stories. When you find yourself grasping, confused, or feeling unworthy, it's powerful to name whatever you're experiencing. Begin to say, "I see you, self-loathing," "I see you, shame," "I see you unworthiness," "I see you, grasping to be someone different," or whatever applies to your experience.

The seeds for awakening weren't unique to the Buddha; they lie within all of us and simply await favorable conditions to flourish. Bringing awareness and acknowledgment to what was formerly unknown and unnamed is like bringing water and light to these seeds; it's a key part of awakening to wisdom and compassion. The light of awareness allows you to recognize grasping and aversion and helps you see through the fog of unawareness so that you can feel more freedom.

~ Jason's Story

Jason began practicing mindfulness meditation because he was unhappy. Early in life, he'd learned that accomplishing goals was the way to be happy and successful, and ever since, he'd pursued this path relentlessly. He excelled in school, graduated with high honors from a top engineering college, and was hired to a great company with a six-figure salary. He married, started a family, got a great car, and acquired all the cool new techno gadgets and toys of the day.

From the outside, all seemed to be well. Jason was a good husband and father, and people were forever complimenting him on his accomplishments. Yet deep within, he had a unsettling, gnawing feeling. He didn't experience much joy in what he had. At first he thought he just needed more, so he continued to buy the latest, greatest, and newest things—a boat, a home theater system, expensive wines, and ultimately a second vacation home. But he still felt adrift and didn't know what to do with his life.

Finally, these feelings led him to a mindfulness-based stress reduction class offered by his company. He was tired of feeling adrift and not enjoying his "successes," and determined to understand more about himself and why he felt the way he did. This was entirely new territory for him, but as an engineer, he reasoned that these pervasive feelings must have an underlying cause.

Several weeks into the mindfulness program, Jason was on a business trip and passed through the town where he had grown up. Although it wasn't like him, he took a long, slow walk in his old neighborhood. He said he felt drawn to walk in his old haunts to see and feel what arose inside him. As he walked by the elementary school he had attended, he saw a young boy, maybe seven years old, playing on the same jungle gym that he had played on decades earlier.

Memories flooded Jason as he walked down his old street and saw the houses of all of his childhood friends, including John, who was just one year older than Jason and had died the year before. Jason walked past his old house and felt like knocking on the door and telling the people who lived there now that it used to be his house, but he settled for just looking around outside. He saw the old brick barbecue that his Dad had built, and this made him quite happy.

Yet that walk through his old neighborhood was also like visiting the ghosts of his past, and many painful memories arose—things he hadn't remembered in many years. Jason remembered being picked on and made fun of, and how other kids didn't like him because he was so brainy and seemed weird to them. He recalled hearing grown-ups talking about who was successful and who wasn't, and how they measured success in terms of having the biggest house, car, or paycheck. He realized that this is where he began to get the idea that success could buy happiness. As he sat with that realization, he recalled making a resolution in childhood that he would show everyone: he would become accomplished and wealthy, and, as a result, very, very happy.

As Jason continued walking down his old street, he felt a willingness to allow these painful feelings to emerge, to acknowledge them, and to let them be—all the deep pains of the past. He allowed himself to feel it all: not being liked, the pain of wanting to be different or special, and the fear that he could never be successful enough to be truly happy. He saw how all of this had created a story that led him to his present discontent, and also realized that he was much more than this old story. This gave him the first feelings of freedom and possibility he'd had in a long time.

In the weeks that followed, Jason began to see things differently. He realized that there was nothing inherently bad about material things and that he could enjoy them, but he also began to see that true happiness comes from within. As he looked back on his childhood struggles, he felt a great deal of compassion for the boy he had been and opened his heart to make peace with himself. And after all of his decades of thinking more is always better, it was incredibly liberating to finally accept himself and his accomplishments as good enough. As Jason felt more connected to himself, he felt more connected to everything and everyone, and his relationships were transformed. When he brought his real, genuine self to his wife, family, friends, and others, his interactions were suffused with a quality of kindness, clarity, and meaning he hadn't imagined possible. His heart broke open and he began to soar with love.

Exercise: "Ah, That Too"

"Ah, that too" is another way of saying, "I see you, Mara." It's a way of fostering the willingness to admit and acknowledge to yourself all of the painful feelings you've been harboring. This acknowledgment can lighten your heavy load.

Begin by bringing awareness to your breath and practicing mindful breathing for a few minutes.

Gently shift your attention and imagine walking through the neighborhood where you once lived. See your old home and your friends' houses. Remember the smell of leaves burning in the fall, dogs barking, crickets chirping on hot summer days—whatever details you associate most strongly with that childhood home. Really immerse yourself in the scene.

Now shift your focus and spend a few minutes reflecting on any painful feelings or memories this visualization of your childhood home may evoke. Sense how you feel in your body, thoughts, and emotions. Whatever feelings you find, just acknowledge them and try to let them be. Use the simple statement "Ah, that too" to help foster a spirit of openness and curiosity about these feelings.

As you welcome these long-disowned feelings, consider whether they offer you a clearer understanding of why you see the world the way you do and why you tend to get stuck in the same stories. And in this very moment, notice how it feels when you become aware of your narrative-based self. How does it affect your experience of your immediacy-based self right now?

Now gently shift into your heart and take a few minutes to honor what you've just reflected upon. It takes courage and vulnerability to open your heart to painful feelings. Bring some tenderness and compassion to yourself.

Return to mindful breathing for a few minutes.

Take some time to write in your journal about your experiences with this exercise. Were you able to access childhood memories? What came up for you physically, mentally, and emotionally? What have you learned from this exploration that you can bring into your life right now?

Which Dog Are You Feeding?

There's an old Native American tale about an elder who felt like he had two dogs living in his head, one mean-spirited and the other sweet, who often fought with one another. Someone once asked him, "Which dog usually wins?" He replied, "It depends on which one I feed."

Can you relate to this story? Which attitudes of mind do you feed? Buddhist psychology offers some very sensible and down-to-earth teachings to help you choose which dog to feed. These are found in the fourth noble truth, the Noble Eightfold Path, which describes eight interrelated elements for awakening. This path is a way of living in the world that helps foster happiness and peace. This path helps promote compassion, wisdom, and, psychologically speaking, stability of mind.

The eight elements of this path are of immense importance in helping to dispel the trance of unworthiness, inadequacy, shame, and all of the related suffering, so we'll take a look at all of them. They are sometimes divided into three aspects that mutually support one another: wisdom, integrity, and concentration. These three aspects are seen as forming a path that begins and ends with wisdom. Wisdom gets you on the path and guides you in how to live your life with more integrity. Integrity, in turn, supports concentration, or training the mind, which allows deeper wisdom to grow. Circling back to wisdom in this way creates a spiral that takes the path into a deeper understanding of the nature of mind and body.

So now let's take a look at the eight elements of the Noble Eightfold Path within these three divisions: wisdom, integrity, and concentration.

Wisdom

Wisdom consists of two elements: wise understanding and wise intention. These vitally important elements awaken you and inspire you to walk on the path to peace. They help you recognize that you reap what you sow and inspire you to begin to turn more inward. Don't think of these qualities, or any of the aspects of the Noble Eightfold Path, as requirements or commandments; rather, look at them as ways of learning how to create less suffering as you live your life. Be compassionate with yourself as you walk this path. There will be times when you will default back to that old, habitual sense of unworthiness, inadequacy, and shame, but the moment you realize this, you're back again, and free from entrapment in your conditioning.

With wise understanding, you begin to see the causes of your sense of shame, inadequacy, and being flawed, and also see that there's a way out. You recognize that, through your thoughts, your mind is the creator of your own heaven and hell. You begin to understand that your actions create reactions, and you try to live in a way that doesn't harm yourself and others.

With wise intention, you learn to let go of clinging and aversion—not because they're morally bad, but because they create suffering in your life. In addition, wise intention informs you and invites you to "feed the good dog" by practicing goodwill, compassion, and loving-kindness and to "starve the mean dog" that spews out judgment, ill will, anger, and unhappiness.

Try the following exercise as a way to develop these qualities.

Exercise: Cultivating Wise Understanding and Intention

For the next week, take some time each day to watch your mind when you experience and react to a stressful or unpleasant event. Notice whether your reaction increases or decreases your sense of ease in your body, thoughts, and emotions.

Over time, notice whether you see any patterns emerging. Do you notice any actions that create feelings of unworthiness, shame, or inadequacy? What can you learn about yourself from these patterns?

Create an intention to avoid causing harm to yourself or others with your thoughts, words, or actions. Notice how following through on this intention makes you feel.

Create an intention to practice goodwill, compassion, and loving-kindness toward yourself and others. Again, notice how following through on this intention makes you feel.

Integrity

As your wise understanding and wise intention grow, you come to recognize the importance of living life with more integrity or virtue. You understand the effects and impacts of your actions on yourself and others. Living with integrity is considered to be a foundational practice for developing concentration or stability of mind, which in turn is essential for wisdom to grow. This is because what we do and how we do it exert a powerful influence on our relationships and how we feel about ourselves. To live with integrity, we need to pay attention to what we say and do, including what we do for a livelihood. Indeed, these are the three elements of the Noble Eightfold Path within the division of integrity: wise speech, wise action, and wise livelihood.

Wise speech is the practice of being mindful of your words and speaking with honesty and kindness in all of your relationships—including your relationship with yourself. This obviously entails avoiding words that hurt feelings and cause pain, such as slander, insults, gossip, or harsh speech. It also includes avoiding meaningless chatter. Speaking unwisely creates disharmony and causes division. When you speak with care, words can heal and create deep connection. Words are powerful and can bless us or scar us. Make it a practice to be mindful of your own self-talk. If it's filled with self-loathing and harsh criticism, notice how this feeds a sense of unworthiness, inadequacy, or shame.

Wise action is important for many reasons, not least because your actions have such an enormous influence on your mood states and relationships. Wise action means living in a way that causes the least harm to yourself and to others. It involves living with integrity, since this supports happiness, contentment, and a quiet mind. The intention is to foster safety for yourself and others by paying close attention to what you do and don't do. Obviously, this means not killing, stealing, or hurting others—physically or emotionally. It also means avoiding alcohol and other intoxicants. If your mind is clouded, it's all the more difficult to practice these intentions and live with integrity.

Wise livelihood could be seen as an extension of wise action. It's important to bring all of those same considerations to what you do for a livelihood and try and find employment that isn't harmful to anyone. At the same time, we acknowledge that this may not be feasible if you're struggling to make ends meet or to find any employment whatsoever. You may not be able to change jobs or find the ideal job at this time, but you can work toward that, and in the meantime you can choose wise action in regard to work and career. Ultimately, you'll find that when your livelihood, your words, and even the smallest of your actions are chosen in service of living with integrity, not only will you benefit, but so will those around you.

Exercise: Cultivating Wise Speech, Wise Action, and Wise Livelihood

This exercise will help you explore your speech, actions, and livelihood. For the next week, we ask that you devote an entire day to each of these facets with the intention of choosing wise speech, wise action, and wise livelihood. As you do so, be like a scientist and see for yourself how acting on these intentions affects you and others throughout the day.

First, choose a day to practice wise speech. On that day, pay close attention to your use of words for the entire day and make a sincere effort to speak with honesty and kindness in all of your communications, including your self-talk. At the end of the day, take some time to write in your journal about what you discovered. How did practicing wise speech make you and others feel?

Next, choose a day to practice wise action. On that day, pay close attention to your actions for the entire day and make a sincere effort to act with kindness and cause no injury to yourself or others. At the end of the day, take some time to write in your journal about what you discovered. How did practicing wise action make you and others feel?

Finally, choose a day to practice wise livelihood. On that day, pay close attention to how you feel doing the work that you do. For the entire day, make an effort to work with kindness and cause no injury to yourself or others. Try to bring respect and kindness to your coworkers and to do your job efficiently and sincerely. Cultivate a spirit of cooperation rather than competition and try to be fair. At the end of the day, take some time to write in your journal about what you discovered. How did practicing wise livelihood make you and others feel?

Concentration

Living with integrity and kindness—including toward yourself—can go a long way toward dissolving pervasive feelings of shame, inadequacy, or unworthiness. These practices of virtuous living cultivate safety and will also help your mind become calmer, clearer, and more capable of concentration—the third division of the Noble Eightfold Path, comprising the elements of wise effort, wise mindfulness, and wise concentration.

Wise effort helps you recognize and restrain states of mind that create suffering. There is no fire hotter than greed, no ice colder than hatred, and no fog thicker than ignorance. With wise effort, you begin to develop and maintain states of mind that, from the perspective of Buddhist psychology, promote awakening: mindfulness, investigation, energy, rapture, tranquility, concentration, and equanimity.

Wise mindfulness is something you've been exploring through much of this book. It's a practice and way of being that allows you to consider, acknowledge, and be with all aspects of your experience. This is the most direct way to get disentangled from the conditioned self. The four foundations of wise mindfulness are awareness of the body, awareness of feeling tones (moment-to-moment experiences of body and mind that are either pleasant, unpleasant, or neutral), awareness of mind states, and awareness of mental objects or phenomena. All four of these forms of awareness will support your awakening and help you understand how to work with the hindrances that come up in meditation. Throughout the book, we've provided practices that develop each of these four interrelated foundations. The body scan, mindful breathing, and bringing mindfulness to daily activities helps develop mindfulness of the body. Being mindful of the feelings tones of any experience in the body and mind helps you become aware of your gut feelings. The practices of being mindful of thoughts and emotions, self-inquiry, and noting help you develop awareness of mind states. And the practice of mindfulness meditation helps you develop awareness of mental objects or phenomena that supports deeper wisdom. While these practices have different focuses, ultimately they are all interconnected and interrelated, and all foster wise mindfulness.

Wise concentration enables you to cultivate a quieter, more tranquil and serene mind. Through the practice of applying your awareness to a single object (such as the breath) and sustaining it there, your mind will grow more one-pointed, and you can experience deeper levels of calm and tranquility.

Exercise: Cultivating Wise Effort, Wise Mindfulness, and Wise Concentration

This exercise will help you explore wise effort, wise mindfulness, and wise concentration over the next week. As with the previous exercise, each day you'll devote the entire day to practicing aspects of these three facets and observing the impact on yourself and others. And as before, at the end of each day take some time to write in your journal about what you experienced as a result of that day's practice.

First, devote two days to practicing wise effort. This involves two steps: The first is recognizing and refraining from states of mind that create suffering, and the second is cultivating states of mind that promote awakening and casting off old, self-limiting definitions.

~ The first day, devote your attention to recognizing and disidentifying with thoughts, emotions, and actions that create suffering in your life.

~ The second day, put a huge amount of intention into promoting thoughts, emotions, and actions that create feelings of happiness and peace.

Next, devote four days to practicing wise mindfulness. Each day you'll attend to one of the four foundations of wise mindfulness: awareness of the body, feeling tones, mind states, and mental objects or phenomena.

~ The first day of this practice, attend to your body throughout the entire day. Be mindful of your posture, how your body engages in your daily activities, and what your body is feeling.

~ Devote the entire second day to being mindful of the feeling tones in your moment-to-moment experience. These are not as fully developed and sophisticated as thoughts and emotions; they're more like gut feelings, and they can fluctuate among being pleasant, unpleasant, and neutral.

~ The third day, attend to mind states throughout the entire day, noticing how thoughts and emotions arise and pass in your awareness. Notice how some thoughts and emotions create feelings of unworthiness and anguish, and others create feelings of happiness and peace.

~ Throughout the fourth day, be mindful of mental objects or phenomena that promote suffering, such as craving, anger, restlessness, sleepiness, and doubt, and, conversely, also notice how mindfulness, tranquility, concentration, and equanimity ease suffering. As this practice develops, you will comprehend more deeply the nature of the body and mind.

On the final day of this practice, cultivate wise concentration by bringing your attention to a single focus and sustaining it there. We suggest that you focus on mindfulness of breathing, doing two thirty-minute practices on this day, sustaining your attention on the breath without wavering as best as possible.

A New Direction

Buddhist psychology asserts that you can escape the confines of the narrative-based self and live within a more mindful, immediacy-based self by practicing wisdom, virtue, and concentration. This is a practical and down-to-earth path, and we hope you adopt it so that you can live with more freedom and joy. Please remember that the word "practice" is exactly fitting here; it's a lifelong journey, and perfection isn't the goal— nor is it possible. There will be times when you fall back into habitual ways of thinking and acting. You may sometimes fall back under the trance of unworthiness. But remember, the moment you become aware that you aren't present, you're present once again. May you practice with kindness, patience, and immense self-compassion.

We each have a birthright to live with more peace and con-nectedness, free from the grip of feeling unworthy, inadequate, and disconnected. Despite how you've suffered in the past, the gifts conferred by this birthright may not be so foreign. Many of us have experienced moments of grace when we felt at one with the world. Perhaps you've had that feeling while just walking down the street or doing something seemingly mundane. Often it feels like time has slowed down and the temperature is just right. You feel completely safe, comfortable, and at ease—and so connected and interconnected that it may not even matter whether you live or die because you feel like you are the universe. It could be as brief as a moment, but it's a precious moment—a moment out of time.

Wouldn't it be amazing to live this way, with mind, body, and heart expanded beyond limited definitions of self? We may not be able to live this way in every moment, but through the practice of mindfulness we can bring more of these moments to our lives. We hope this book has helped you do just that, and that as you travel this path, you come to live with your heart wide open. D. H. Lawrence captured this experience well in his poem "Escape" (1993, 482):

> When we get out of the glass bottles of our own ego,
> and when we escape like squirrels from turning in the cages
>   of our personality
> and get into the forest again,
> we shall shiver with cold and fright
> but things will happen to us
> so that we don't know ourselves.
> Cool, unlying life will rush in,
> and passion will make our bodies taut with power,
> we shall stamp our feet with new power
> and old things will fall down,
> we shall laugh, and institutions will curl up like burnt paper.

Mindfulness Practice: Integration Meditation

We'd like to leave you with a closing meditation to help integrate everything you've learned as you've worked with this book, and to support you in your journey forward. Take as long as you like with this meditation, and linger with each element of it however long you wish.

> Sit or lie comfortably and take a few moments to become mindful of your breathing. No effort is needed, just let the breath happen as it will. Be mindful of your body breathing you. You and the breath, the winds of life, so precious and fragile.
>
> Take this moment to appreciate who you are, imperfectly perfect as you are—the good, the bad, and the ugly, along with the ten thousand joys and sorrows. Letting it all in, and letting it all be... Observing and allowing whatever you experience...
>
> Watch how your stories come and go like the wind, ever ephemeral and transient. There's no need to fix them or do anything. Just observe, allow, and let them be.
>
> You will gradually come to understand the nature of all things.
>
> Opening to the heart of compassion and loving-kindness for yourself...
>
> Opening to the heart of compassion and loving-kindness for the world...
>
> Opening to the heart of compassion and loving-kindness for the universe...
>
> May all beings be safe.
>
> May all beings be at ease.
>
> May all beings dwell in peace.

~

Resources

Recommended Readings on Mindfulness

Analayo. 2002. *Satipatthana: The Direct Path to Realization*. Birmington, UK: Windhorse.

Bennett-Goleman, T. 2001. *Emotional Alchemy: How the Mind Can Heal the Heart*. Random House. New York.

Brach, T. 2004. *Radical Acceptance*. New York: Bantam.

Brantley, J. 2007. *Calming Your Anxious Mind: How Mindfulness and Compassion Can Free You from Anxiety, Fear, and Panic*. Oakland, CA: New Harbinger Publications.

Chödrön, P. 2000. *When Things Fall Apart*. Boston: Shambhala.

———. 2007. *The Places That Scare You*. Boston: Shambhala.

Dalai Lama. 1998. "Training the Mind: Verse 1." www.dalailama.com.

Dalai Lama and H. C. Cutler. 1998. *The Art of Happiness: A Handbook for Living*. New York: Riverhead Books.

Epstein, M. 1995. *Thoughts Without a Thinker*. New York: Perseus Group.

———. 2001. *Going on Being: Life at the Crossroads of Buddhism and Psychotherapy.* New York: Broadway Books.

Flowers, S. 2009. *The Mindful Path Through Shyness.* Oakland, CA: New Harbinger Publications.

Goldstein, J. 1983. *The Experience of Insight.* Boston: Shambhala.

———. 2003. *Insight Meditation: The Practice of Freedom.* Boston: Shambhala.

———. 2003. *One Dharma: The Emerging Western Buddhism.* San Francisco: Harper.

Goldstein, J., and J. Kornfield. 2001. *Seeking the Heart of Wisdom.* Boston: Shambhala.

Gunaratana, H. 2002. *Mindfulness in Plain English.* Boston: Wisdom.

Hanson, R., and R. Mendius. 2009. *Buddha's Brain: The Practical Neuroscience of Happiness, Love, and Wisdom.* Oakland, CA. New Harbinger Publications.

Kabat-Zinn, J. 1990. *Full Catastrophe Living.* New York: Delta.

———. 1994. *Wherever You Go, There You Are.* New York: Hyperion.

———. 2005. *Coming to Our Senses.* New York: Hyperion.

———. 2007. *Arriving at Your Own Door: 108 Lessons in Mindfulness.* New York: Hyperion.

Kornfield, J. 1993. *A Path with Heart: A Guide Through the Perils and Promises of Spiritual Life.* New York: Bantam.

———. 2000. *After the Ecstasy, the Laundry.* New York: Bantam.

———. 2008. *The Wise Heart.* New York: Bantam.

Levey, J., and M. Levey. 2009. *Luminous Mind: Meditation and Mind Fitness.* San Francisco: Red Wheel.

Nhat Hanh, T. 1996. *The Miracle of Mindfulness.* Boston: Beacon.

———. 2005. *Being Peace.* Berkeley, CA: Parallax Press.

Nyanaponika. 1973. *The Heart of Buddhist Meditation.* Boston: Weiser Books.

Rahula, W. 1974. *What the Buddha Taught*. New York: Grove Press.

Rosenberg, L. 1998. *Breath by Breath: The Liberating Practice of Insight Meditation*. Boston: Shambhala.

————. 2000. *Living in the Light of Death*. Boston: Shambhala.

Salzberg, S. 1997. *Lovingkindness: The Revolutionary Art of Happiness*. Boston: Shambhala.

Santorelli, S. 1999. *Heal Thyself: Lessons in Mindfulness in Medicine*. New York: Three Rivers Press.

Shunryu, S. 1970. *Zen Mind, Beginner's Mind*. New York. Weatherhill.

Siegel, D. 2007. *The Mindful Brain: Reflections and Attunement in the Cultivation of Well-Being*. New York: W. W. Norton.

Stahl, B., and E. Goldstein. 2010. *A Mindfulness-Based Stress Reduction Workbook*. Oakland, CA: New Harbinger Publications.

Sumedho, A. 1995. *The Mind and the Way*. Boston: Wisdom.

————. 2007. *The Sound of Silence*. Boston: Wisdom.

Trungpa, C. 1991. *Meditation in Action*. Boston: Shambhala.

Poetry and Inspirational Writing

Eliot, T. S. 1963. *Collected Poems*. Orlando, FL: Harcourt Brace.

Gibran, K. 1923. *The Prophet*. New York. Alfred Knopf.

Hafiz. 1999. *The Gift*. Translated by D. Ladinsky. New York: Penguin Group.

Kabir. 2004. *Kabir: Ecstatic Poems*. Translated by R. Bly. Boston: Beacon.

Kafka, F. 1946. *The Great Wall of China and Other Pieces*. London: Secker and Warburg.

Lawrence, D. H.1993. *Complete Poems*. New York. Penguin.

Nelson, P. 1993. *There's a Hole in My Sidewalk: The Romance of Self-Discovery*. Hillsboro, OR: Beyond Words.

Oman, M. (ed.). 2000. *Prayers for Healing: 365 Blessings, Poems, and Meditations from Around the World.* Berkeley, CA: Conari Press.

Rumi. 1987. *We Are Three.* Translated by C. Barks. Athens, GA: Maypop.

———. 1995. *The Essential Rumi.* Translated by C. Barks with J. Moyne. San Francisco: HarperCollins.

———. 1997. *The Illuminated Rumi.* Translated by C. Barks. New York: Broadway Books.

———. 1999. *Open Secret.* Translated by J. Moyne and C. Barks. Boston: Shambhala.

———. 2002. *The Soul of Rumi.* Translated by C. Barks. San Francisco: HarperCollins.

———. 2006. *A Year with Rumi.* Translated by C. Barks. San Francisco: HarperCollins.

Stafford, W. 1998. *The Way It Is.* St. Paul, MN: Graywolf Press.

Mindfulness Audio and Video Resources

Mindfulness Meditation CDs by Bob Stahl

To purchase or listen to a sample of these CDs and DVDs, visit www .yourheartwideopen.com or www.mindfulnessprograms.com/mindful-healing-series.html.

Audio Recordings

~ *Opening to Change, Forgiveness, and Loving-Kindness*

~ *Working with Chronic Pain*

~ *Working with Neck and Shoulder Pain*

~ *Working with Back Pain*

~ *Working with Insomnia and Sleep Challenges*

~ *Working with Anxiety, Fear, and Panic*

~ *Working with High Blood Pressure*

~ *Working with Heart Disease*

~ *Working with Headaches and Migraines*

~ *Working with Asthma, COPD, and Respiratory Challenges*

~ *Body Scan and Sitting Meditation*

~ *Lying and Standing Yoga*

~ *Impermanence and Loving-Kindness Meditation*

Video Recordings

~ *Mindful Qigong and Loving-Kindness Meditation*

Mindfulness Meditation CDs and DVDs by Steve Flowers

To purchase or listen to a sample of these CDs, DVDs, and digital files, visit www.yourheartwideopen.com or www.mindfullivingprograms .com.

Audio Recordings

~ *Body Scan and Yoga Meditation*

~ *Sitting Meditation and Qigong Meditation*

~ *Loving-Kindness and Self-Compassion Meditation*

~ *Reconciliation and Forgiveness Meditation*

Video Recordings

~ *Qigong and Yoga Meditation*

~ *Watercourse Meditation: Soothing Water Imagery and Guided Meditation for Stress Reduction*

~ *Loving-Kindness and Forgiveness Meditation*

Mindfulness Resources

Mindfulness-Based Stress-Reduction Programs

Mindfulness-Based Stress Reduction programs abound throughout the United States as well as internationally. If you're interested in joining a program near you, check out the regional and international directory at the Center for Mindfulness at University of Massachusetts Medical School's website: www.umassmed.edu/cfm/mbsr.

Opening Your Heart Retreats: www.yourheartwideopen.com.

Mindful Living Programs: www.mindfullivingprograms.com. Offers retreats, including accredited continuing education retreats for medical and mental health professionals, at several locations in California.

Awareness and Relaxation Training: www.mindfulnessprograms.com. Offers retreats in the San Francisco Bay Area.

Insight Meditation Society: www.dharma.org/ims. Offers retreats in Massachusetts.

Spirit Rock Meditation Center: www.spiritrock.org. Offers retreats in the San Francisco Bay Area.

Gaia House: www.gaiahouse.co.uk. Offers retreats in the South Devon countryside.

References

Amaro, A. 2010. Back cover copy. *Inquiring Mind* 26(2): back cover.

Analayo. 2003. *Satipatthana: The Direct Path to Realization*. Birmington, UK: Windhorse.

Bennett-Goleman, T. 2001. *Emotional Alchemy: How the Mind Can Heal the Heart*. New York: Random House.

Bowlby, J. 1988. *A Secure Base: Parent-Child Attachment and Healthy Human Development*. New York: Basic Books.

Brach, T. 2004. *Radical Acceptance*. New York: Bantam.

Bradshaw, J. 1988. *Healing the Shame That Binds You*. Deerfield Beach, FL: Health Communications.

Brown, E. E. 2009. *The Complete Tassajara Cookbook: Recipes, Techniques, and Reflections from the Famed Zen Kitchen*. Boston: Shambhala.

Cerf, B. A. 1948. *Shake Well Before Using: A New Collection of Impressions and Anecdotes, Mostly Humorous*. New York: Simon and Schuster.

Dalai Lama and H. C. Cutler. 1998. *The Art of Happiness: A Handbook for Living*. New York: Riverhead Books.

Dalai Lama and P. Ekman. 2008. *Emotional Awareness: Overcoming the Obstacles to Psychological Balance and Compassion*. New York: Times Books.

Davidson, R. J. 2009. Keynote address at the fourth annual scientific conference: Investigating and Integrating Mindfulness in Medicine, Health Care, and Society, Worcester, MA.

Davidson, R. J., J. Kabat-Zinn, J. Schumacher, M. Rosenkranz, D. Muller, S. F. Santorelli, F. Urbanowski, A. Harrington, K. Bonus, and J. F. Sheridan. 2003. Alterations in brain and immune function produced by mindfulness meditation. *Psychosomatic Medicine* 65(4):564-570.

Einhorn, L. 1991. *Forgiveness and Child Abuse: Would You Forgive?* Bandon, OR: Robert D. Reed.

Einstein, A. 1972. Letter quoted in the *New York Post*. November 28, p. 12.

Ellis, A. 1969. Sex, sanity, and psychotherapy (cassette recording). New York: Institute for Rational Emotive Therapy.

Farb, N. A, Z. V. Segal, H. Mayberg, J. Bean, D. McKeon, Z. Fatima, and A. K. Anderson. 2007. Attending to the present: Mindfulness meditation reveals distinct neural modes of self-reference. *Social, Cognitive, and Affective Neuroscience* 2(4): 313-322.

Fénelon, F. 2002. *The Spiritual Letters of Archbishop Fénelon: Letters to Women*. Translated by H. L. S. Lear. London: Longmans, Green, and Co.

Frager, R., and J. Fadiman (eds.). 1999. *Essential Sufism*. New York: HarperCollins.

Ghose, S. 1991. *Mahatma Gandhi*. Bombay: Allied Publishers.

Gilbert, P., and S. Proctor. 2006. Compassionate mind training for people with high shame and self-criticism: Overview and pilot study of a group therapy approach. *Clinical Psychology and Psychotherapy* 13(6):353-379.

Goldstein, J. 2003. *One Dharma: The Emerging Western Buddhism*. San Francisco: Harper.

Goleman, D. 2003. *Healing Emotions: Conversations with the Dalai Lama on Mindfulness, Emotions, and Health*. Boston: Shambhala.

Hanson, R., and R. Mendius. 2009. *Buddha's Brain: The Practical Neuroscience of Happiness, Love, and Wisdom*. Oakland, CA: New Harbinger Publications.

Harlow, H. F. 1959. Love in infant monkeys. *Scientific American* 200(6):68-74.

James, W. 1890. *The Principles of Psychology*. New York: Henry-Holt and Co.

Killingsworth, M. A., and D. T. Gilbert. 2010. A wandering mind is an unhappy mind. *Science* 330(6606):932.

King, M. L., Jr. 1992. Nobel Prize acceptance speech (1964), in *I Have a Dream: Writings and Speeches That Changed the World*. New York: Harper Collins.

Kornfield, J. 1993. *A Path with Heart: A Guide Through the Perils and Promises of Spiritual Life*. New York: Bantam Books.

Lawrence, D. H. 1993. *Complete Poems*. New York: Penguin Classics.

Luskin, F. 2010. The choice to forgive. In *The Compassionate Instinct: The Science of Human Goodness*. Edited by D. Keltner, J. Marsh, and J. Smith. New York: W. W. Norton.

Narada Thera (translator). 2004. *The Dhammapada*. Whitefish, MT: Kessinger Publications.

Neff, K. D., and P. McGehee. 2008. Self-compassion among adolescents and young adults. Paper presented at the 38th annual meeting of the Jean Piaget Society, Quebec City, Canada.

Oman, M. (ed.). 2000. *Prayers for Healing: 365 Blessings, Poems, and Meditations from Around the World*. Berkeley, CA: Conari Press.

Pattakos, A. 2008. *Prisoners of Our Thoughts: Viktor Frankl's Principles for Discovering Meaning in Life and Work*. San Francisco: Berrett-Koehler.

Rumi. 1995. *The Essential Rumi*. Translated by C. Barks with J. Moyne. New York: HarperCollins.

Rumi. 1997. *The Illuminated Rumi*. Translated by C. Barks. New York: Broadway Books.

Rumi. 2010. *Rumi: The Big Red Book: The Great Masterpiece Celebrating Mystical Love and Friendship*. Translated by C. Banks. New York: Harper Collins.

Siegel, D. 2007. *The Mindful Brain: Reflections and Attunement in the Cultivation of Well-Being*. New York: W. W. Norton.

Siegel, R. 2010. *The Neurobiology of Mindfulness: Clinical Applications*. Teleconference, National Institute of the Clinical Application of Behavioral Medicine.

Stahl, B., and E. Goldstein. 2010. *A Mindfulness-Based Stress Reduction Workbook*. Oakland, CA: New Harbinger Publications.

Thoreau, H. D. 2006. *Thoreau and the Art of Life: Precepts and Principles*. Edited by R. MacIver. North Ferrisberg, VT: Heron Dance Press.

Trungpa, C. 1991. *Meditation in Action*. Boston: Shambhala.

Wheatley, M. 1999. Consumed by either fire or fire: Journeying with T. S. Eliot. *Journal of Noetic Science*, November, 1-5.

Williams, M. 1922. *The Velveteen Rabbit, or, How Toys Became Real*. New York: Doran.

Winnicott, D. W. 1996. *Maturational Processes and the Facilitating Environment*. London: Karnac Books.

Steve Flowers, MFT, founded the mindfulness-based stress reduction (MBSR) program at Enloe Medical Center and pioneered the international MBSR online program. With Bob Stahl, he leads mindful-living programs and mindfulness retreats for medical and health professionals, couples, and individuals seeking to cultivate mindfulness and compassion in their lives. Directing and providing wellness programs and workshops for corporations, city and county governments, medical centers, and universities, he is deeply committed to bringing mindfulness into health care and society.

Bob Stahl, PhD, founded and directs mindfulness-based stress reduction (MBSR) programs in three medical centers in the San Francisco Bay Area. A longtime mindfulness practitioner who lived in a Buddhist monastery for over eight years, he serves as an adjunct senior teacher at Oasis, the institute for mindfulness-based professional education and innovation at the Center for Mindfulness in Medicine, Health Care, and Society at the University of Massachusetts Medical School. He is coauthor of *A Mindfulness-Based Stress Reduction Workbook.*

Foreword writer **Tara Brach, PhD,** has been practicing meditation since 1975 and leads Buddhist meditation retreats at centers throughout North America. She is a clinical psychologist and author of *Radical Acceptance* and *True Refuge.*

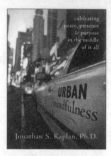

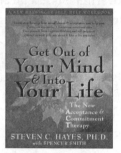